W9-CRN-221

OSPREY
PUBLISHING

23rd Fighter Group
'Chennault's Sharks'

OSPREY
PUBLISHING

23rd Fighter Group
'Chennault's Sharks'

Carl Molesworth

Series editor Tony Holmes

Front Cover

P-51As and P-40Ks of the 76th FS/ 23rd FG had a fierce encounter with Ki-43-IIs of the 11th and 25th Sentais near the airfield at Suichuan, in China, on 27 December 1943. The 76th FS, led by its newly appointed commanding officer Capt John S Stewart, had only moved from Kweilin to the advanced base at Suichuan, on the Kan River in Kiangsi Province, 24 hours earlier. Japanese intelligence was clearly very good in this area, as the Japanese Army Air Force's 3rd Air Division launched an attack on the base from Canton the very next morning.

Seven P-51As and seven P-40Ks scrambled at 1130 hrs upon receiving word of approaching enemy aircraft via the warning net. At about 1145 hrs, six Ki-48 'Lily' bombers made a run over the base from south to north at 1500 ft, destroying a B-25 in a revetment and the 76th FS's alert shack. Meanwhile, Capt Stewart led his mixed fighter formation in an attack on the escorting Ki-43 'Oscars' at 12,000 ft directly overhead the base. A tremendous fight then ensued, after which Stewart claimed one 'Oscar' probably destroyed. All but one of his pilots submitted claims following the engagement, five of which were for the destruction of Ki-43 fighters. This was an unusually accurate tally for the CBI, as the 25th Sentai had indeed lost three 'Oscars' and the 11th Sentai one.

Among the Japanese pilots killed was Capt Nakakazu Ozaki, a 19-victory ace and commander of the 2nd Chutai/25th Sentai. He crashed ten kilometres southwest of Suichuan. The Japanese in turn claimed ten victories, but the only 76th aircraft lost was the P-40K flown by Lt Robert Schaeffer. The latter subsequently reported what had happened to him;

'I was in P-40 No 112, rolling straight down on a Zero's tail when I felt the engine jump. I looked down at my manifold pressure gauge, which started dropping, and realised I was hit. So I dove away to the east on the deck. I tried to use the throttle and prop controls, but both were useless. The fight was still going on over the field, and as I had only 20 inches Hg (mercury) showing, I decided I would have to sit down someplace. I picked out a sandbar in the river, cut the engine with the mixture control, pumped down full flaps and bellied in. I overshot a bit and bounced off an eight-foot bank onto another sandbar.'

Unhurt, Schaeffer quickly made contact with some friendly Chinese locals, who in turn helped the Warhawk pilot find his way back to Suichuan air base the following day (*Cover artwork by Mark Postlethwaite*)

First published in Great Britain in 2009 by Osprey Publishing
Midland House, West Way, Botley, Oxford OX2 0PH, UK
443 Park Avenue South, New York, NY 10016, USA
E-mail; info@ospreypublishing.com

A CIP catalogue record for this book is available from the British Library

Print ISBN 978 1 84603 421 3
PDF e-book ISBN 978 1 84603 884 6

Edited by Tony Holmes
Page design by Mark Holt
Cover artwork by Mark Postlethwaite
Aircraft Profiles by Jim Laurier
Index by Alan Thatcher
Originated by PDQ Digital Media Solutions, Suffolk, UK
Printed and bound in China through Bookbuilders

09 10 11 12 13   10 9 8 7 6 5 4 3 2 1

FOR A CATALOGUE OF ALL BOOKS PUBLISHED BY OSPREY MILITARY AND AVIATION PLEASE CONTACT:
Osprey Direct, C/O Random House Distribution Center, 400 Hahn Road, Westminster, MD 21157
E-mail; uscustomerservice@ospreypublishing.com

ALL OTHER REGIONS
Osprey Direct, The Book Service Ltd, Distribution Centre, Colchester Road, Frating Green, Colchester, Essex, CO7 7DW, UK
E-mail; customerservice@ospreypublishing.com

The Woodland Trust
Osprey Publishing are supporting the Woodland Trust, the UK's leading woodland conservation charity, by funding the dedication of trees.

www.ospreypublishing.com

CONTENTS

INTRODUCTION

Although overshadowed in history by its forebear, the American Volunteer Group (AVG), the USAAF's 23rd Fighter Group (FG) made arguably the largest contribution toward the Allied victory in the China-Burma-India (CBI) Theatre of any air unit in World War 2. According to the official USAF website, the 23d FG accounted for the destruction of 621 enemy aeroplanes in air combat and 320 more on the ground. The group sank more than 131,000 tons of enemy shipping and damaged another 250,000 tons. Finally, the 23rd caused an estimated enemy troop loss of more than 20,000 men.

These statistics were compiled during the course of 24,000+ combat sorties totalling more than 53,000 flying hours, and at a cost of 110 aircraft lost in aerial combat – 90 shot down by surface defences and 28 destroyed while parked on the ground.

By the author's count, 32 aces scored five or more victories flying with the 23rd, and eight more claimed at least one victory with the group. Pilots do not compile statistics like these by themselves, however. It takes a complete team effort, with a large staff of ground personnel supporting flight operations. Many of these men served in China for more than three years before they were able to return home, and their skills and devotion to duty cannot be overstated.

Just as important as the 23rd FG's outstanding combat record was its development, and employment, of fighter-bomber tactics, which have

Shown here in the autumn of 1942, these four key pilots of the 75th FS/23rd FG were credited with shooting down a total of nearly 30 Japanese aircraft between them during the course of the war. They are, from left, Capt John R Alison, Maj David L 'Tex' Hill, Capt Albert J 'Ajax' Baumler and Lt Mack A Mitchell. The P-40E behind them displays the unofficial unit badge of the 23rd FG (*Bruce Holloway*)

This handsome P-51D was assigned to Lt Col Bruce C Downs, the very last wartime commander of the 74th FS. The squadron badge shows a gorilla riding a pony. Downs had flown in the RAF's No 121 'Eagle' Sqn earlier in the war, and he also participated in the defence of Malta, prior to transferring to the USAAF in September 1942 (*John Conn*)

served as a model for USAF tactical operations ever since. But the 23rd FG did even more than that, as its pilots flew weather reconnaissance, photo-reconnaissance and even combat cargo missions, the latter seeing drop tanks filled with ammunition and supplies delivered to Chinese troops under siege at Changsha and Hengyang during 1944.

Every year, veterans of the 23rd FG who served in China meet for a reunion. The turnout thins a little at each gathering, but in the peak years it was not unusual for more than 100 personnel to show up. For a few days they peel back 60+ years of bark and return to the core of their lives – the pivotal time they shared in China. The bar opens early and stays open late, with no money changing hands. Voices rise in laughter as old stories are retold for the umpteenth time. Hands swoop and dive when the pilots describe air battles of long ago.

I was lucky enough to attend one of these reunions in October 1991, when the 23rd FG veterans met at Fort Walton Beach, Florida. On a warm afternoon I stood with them on the field at nearby Eglin Air Force Base and watched two menacing-looking jet aircraft performing aerobatics in the sky above. Eventually, the jets landed and began to taxi toward the crowd. As they drew closer, it was clear to see that the dark-green A-10 Thunderbolts were sporting a familiar decoration on their noses – a leering sharksmouth and eyes. Like the veterans in the audience, these jets and their pilots had experienced combat. Earlier that year, when US military forces helped eject the Iraqi military from Kuwait, the 23rd FG had gone back into action as a key unit in Operation *Desert Storm*.

Much of the material contained in this book, and my previous work on the 23rd FG, *Sharks Over China*, is the result of the cooperation and support that I received from the veterans of the 23rd FG at that 1991 reunion. I have stayed in touch with many of them over the years, and I am proud to consider these men my friends and my heroes. I hope they consider my efforts in chronicling the history of the 23rd FG a worthy tribute to the sacrifices that they made for their country at a time when the future of freedom and democracy was on the line around the world.

AVG PASSES THE BATON

War news filled the Sunday papers across the United States on 1 March 1942, and for the most part none of it was good. It was just 11 weeks since the surprise Japanese attack on Pearl Harbor, and the nation was reeling from reports of one setback after another on the Allied war fronts. In the North African desert, Allied and Axis forces were stalemated at Gazala. In the USSR, German troops were laying siege at Leningrad. In northern Europe, Luftwaffe bombers continued to pound London from bases in occupied France.

If anything, the news was even worse from the Pacific. As the US Navy struggled to recover from the pounding it had taken at Pearl Harbor, American ground forces were retreating in the face of the Japanese advance in the Philippines. Singapore had fallen two weeks earlier, and Japanese forces were landing in Java. The first Japanese air raids against northern Australia had also just begun.

The situation was just a little better in Burma (now Myanmar), where a group of American fighter pilots had been attracting worldwide attention since December for their spirited defence of the great port city of Rangoon (Yangon) against Japanese bombing attacks. Commanded by a retired US Army Air Corps (USAAC) captain by the name of Claire Lee Chennault, the AVG consisted of civilian pilots and groundcrews secretly recruited from US military units in 1941 to fly 100 export models of the Curtiss P-40 fighter for China. Their mission was to defend 'The Burma Road', the last supply route into China, from Japanese air attacks.

Flying from newly captured airfields in Thailand, Japanese bombers, with strong fighter escort, first attacked Rangoon on 23 and 25 December 1941 – less than a week after their first bloody encounter with the AVG over Kunming, China. The AVG's 3rd Pursuit Squadron (PS), along with the RAF's No 67 Sqn, flying American-built Brewster Buffaloes, intercepted both raids with great success. In two days, the 3rd PS claimed no fewer than 35 victories, firmly establishing the AVG's glowing reputation. *Time* magazine soon tagged the AVG with the nickname 'The Flying Tigers', and a legend was in the making. When photographs of the AVG's sharkmouthed Tomahawk fighters started appearing in the press, the American public's interest and affection grew.

The AVG continued to fight over Rangoon for two months, but despite its successes, British and colonial ground forces were unable to halt the Japanese advance into Burma. The American press would not report until much later that the last AVG Tomahawks had evacuated Rangoon on 1 March 1942.

Back in the United States, a seemingly unremarkable event took place on 1 March 1942, when the USAAC activated the headquarters section of the newly forming 23rd Pursuit Group (PG) at Langley Field, Virginia.

Maj Gen Claire L Chennault, legendary commander of the China Air Task Force and later the Fourteenth Air Force, is credited with developing the tactics and strategies that the 23rd FG and other units under his command used so successfully against Japanese forces in China during World War 2 (*Ray Crowell*)

The American military had been building up at a frantic pace for more than a year as the prospects of war became increasingly likely. Newly minted pursuit groups were in training throughout the US, and at first glance the 23rd appeared to be destined to join them in preparing for combat. But from the very beginning, this unit was destined to be different, as subsequent events would soon show.

Maj Robert A Culbertson, a broad-shouldered, grey-haired career officer, was assigned as the group's first commander. He and his small cadre of experienced officers and NCOs were given about 100 recruits drawn from other units at Langley and told to get them ready to ship out for overseas in short order. Some of the recruits had joined the Army just a few days earlier, and had not even experienced the 'pleasures' of basic training. Within a week an advance detail under the command of MSgt Clyde Casto went to Charleston, South Carolina, to secure the supplies and equipment that the group would need to take overseas. The rest of the 23rd arrived a week later at Charleston's Overseas Discharge and Replacement Center with orders to ship out immediately for foreign assignment. The group had still not yet been organised into squadrons because it had neither pilots nor aircraft.

23rd PG personnel boarded the converted ocean liner USS *Brazil* during the evening of 17 March 1942, and the ship left Charleston's harbour at 0600 hrs the next morning. Its destination was unknown to the men of the group, who made up but a small number of the 6500 troops embarked in the vessel. A B-25 medium bomber patrolled overhead in the cool morning air as the ship made its way on a zigzag course toward San Juan, Puerto Rico. On board the ship, the men found themselves in cramped quarters. They stood in long lines at chow time and had little to do for the rest of the day. After a quick stop without shore leave at San Juan, USS *Brazil*, along with an escort cruiser and a small aircraft carrier loaded with scout biplanes, headed out across the Atlantic Ocean.

Squadron Leader Robert Neale flew H-81 Tomahawk '7' as commander of the AVG's 1st Pursuit Squadron during 1941-42. Neale served as temporary commander of the 23rd FG for the first two weeks after the unit was activated in July 1942, although technically he was a civilian at the time (*Jack Cook*)

A few days later the convoy arrived at Freetown, in Sierra Leone, on the western coast of Africa. Again the men were prevented from taking shore leave, but they found a diversion in counting the nearly 200 ships in the harbour and watching RAF fighters patrolling overhead.

When USS *Brazil* docked at Cape Town, in South Africa, on 18 April, the men happily set foot on dry land for the first time in a month. From there, the ship rounded the Cape of Good Hope and made another short stop at Port Elizabeth, before setting out on the final leg of the journey. After passing through the Mozambique Straits between Madagascar and Africa, the convoy headed north through the Indian Ocean to dock at Karachi, in India (now Pakistan) on 17 May 1942. Soon the men of the

WAR IN CHINA

World War 2 in Asia was already more than ten years old when the Japanese attacked Pearl Harbor on 7 December 1941 and drew the United States into the conflict. Japan's aggression began in September 1931 with the island nation's capture of Mukden in northeast China. By early 1932 the entire province of Manchuria – China's mineral and industrial heart – was under Japanese control. Infrequent clashes occurred between Japanese and Chinese troops throughout the mid-1930s, despite treaty terms limiting Japan to the areas north of the Great Wall. Then in 1937 open warfare between Japan and China resumed.

Fearing that rival Nationalist and Communist forces in China were about to merge, which could render the nation too strong to subdue by force, the Japanese army incited an exchange of gunfire with Chinese troops at the Marco Polo Bridge near Peking on 7 July 1937. Within a matter of days, Japanese ground forces began pouring into China and a full-scale war was under way. The fighting went badly for the Chinese forces under Generalissimo Chiang Kai-shek. Peking fell quickly, followed by Nanking in December 1937 and then the major port of Canton and city of Hankow in October 1938. Hainan Island in the South China Sea was invaded in February 1939, by which time most active resistance on the Chinese mainland had ceased.

Japan then turned its attention back to Manchuria, where it fought a bitter engagement against the Soviet Union from May to September 1939.

Chiang retreated deep into western China, setting up his capital at Chungking, in Szechuan Province, and millions of Chinese refugees followed him there. Japan now occupied all major Chinese seaports and transportation hubs throughout eastern China. Chiang was cut off from the outside world, except for a thin thread of a supply line that ran from the British-controlled port of Rangoon 800 miles through Burma and onto its terminus at Kunming, in southwest China. The route would soon become known worldwide as 'The Burma Road'.

The Chinese Air Force (CAF) had made a respectable showing during the early fighting against the invaders, flying aircraft imported from the United States, the Soviet Union, Italy and elsewhere. A key element in its sporadic success was the influence of retired USAAC pilot Capt Claire Lee Chennault, who came to China in 1937 to serve as Director of Combat Training for the CAF. He set up flying schools, advised Chiang on aircraft purchases and devised an air-raid warning system. According to some sources, Chennault also flew reconnaissance missions and may have engaged in aerial combat against the Japanese, although his combat record has never been confirmed.

Eventually, the CAF was overwhelmed by the increasing numbers of modern combat aircraft that Japan committed to its war against China. A series of air raids against Chungking began in April 1940, and soon a new Imperial Japanese Navy fighter type, the Mitsubishi A6M Zero-sen, mopped up what was left of the CAF's air defences. By that time, however, Chennault had gained a wealth of knowledge about the capabilities of Japanese aircraft, as well as the strategies and tactics employed by Japanese airmen and their leaders. Stirred by the wanton destruction the Chinese had suffered at the hands of the Japanese, Chennault was determined to put this information to good use. In October 1940, he

23rd Fighter Group (the unit's designation had been changed from 'pursuit' to 'fighter' in orders dated 15 May 1942) made their way through the city to the New Malir Cantonment, on the edge of the nearby Sind Desert.

New Malir was a huge airfield with very little on it, save a cavernous hangar that had originally been built to house a British dirigible. The 23rd FG was assigned to 'C Area', and lived in a scattering of block buildings. It was dusty, boring and extremely hot. Soon, however, Sgt Roy Sell had an excellent mess hall operation going, which improved life quite a bit. Meanwhile, SSgt Edwin Jones organised sports activities that gave the men a chance to blow off some steam. But for now the 23rd FG remained

An extensive system of civilian spotters behind enemy lines provided early warning of incoming Japanese air raids. On the airfields of the 23rd FG, personnel could assess the threat by watching the number of paper balls that were run up a pole near the operations office. A two-ball alert, as shown here at Kweilin, meant enemy aircraft were approaching the base and interceptors should scramble – a third ball signified an attack was imminent (*Tom Raleigh*)

traveled to Washington, D.C., to work with Chinese ambassador T V Soong on selling the United States a new plan for bolstering China's air defences. The result of that trip was the formation of the AVG in the summer of 1941.

A key part of Chennault's grand plan was the maintenance of an air-raid warning net throughout his area of operations. The net was a complex web of ground observers, many of them Chinese civilians, arranged in a grid pattern and linked by telephone and radio. Chennault had begun setting up the warning net soon after arriving in China in 1937, and by 1942 many of the observers in eastern China were located behind enemy lines. Under the direction of

radio expert John Williams, the net was greatly expanded in 1940 so that the information could be fed into command centres where intercept directors could lead Chennault's fighters to approaching Japanese formations.

It was said that the net worked so well that when Japanese aircraft took off from their bases around Hankow, Chennault would know about it within minutes in Kunming, some 800 miles away. Only on rare occasions did the net fail to give advance warning of enemy air raids. His confidence in the net allowed Chennault to spread his meagre forces to advanced airfields near enemy lines with little fear of having them caught on the ground and destroyed.

a paper organisation without pilots or aeroplanes. Events were unfolding elsewhere, however, that would soon change this situation.

In China, the AVG had continued to build on its reputation during the 23rd's two-month sea voyage. In action over Burma and southwest China against the invading Japanese forces, AVG pilots racked up success after success over enemy aircraft and ground targets. But the AVG's status as a civilian organisation was proving problematic for Army 'brass' in Washington, D.C.. If this rowdy bunch could go toe-to-toe with the Japanese, why were regular Army fighter outfits having such a tough time of it in the Philippines and the South Pacific? There was more perception than reality behind this thinking, but the image of the AVG as an embarrassment to the USAAF held sway nevertheless.

The remedy for the situation seemed simple. Inducting the AVG into the Army lock, stock and barrel would legitimise its exploits, and allow the USAAF to claim its future successes. Viewed in this light, it becomes obvious why the 23rd FG was sent to a war zone without aircraft or trained pilots and groundcrews – the men and aeroplanes were already in China fighting the war.

In war, some strategies work and others do not. The induction of the AVG was one that did not. Chennault accepted induction into the Army with the rank of full colonel in April 1942, and began meeting with AVG personnel to urge them to follow his lead. But most of the men were by now thoroughly war-weary, and many of them were ill to boot. They had signed up to fight for a year, and the bulk of them were fixed on the date 4 July 1942, when their contracts with China would expire and they could

Sgt D E Westlake and Chinese assistants work on the hydraulic system and landing gear of a P-40E wing at Kunming Factory No 10. With the landing gear fairing removed, the details of the strut's retraction system are visible. A mix of Tomahawk and Kittyhawk fuselages line the wall in the background (*Bruce Holloway*)

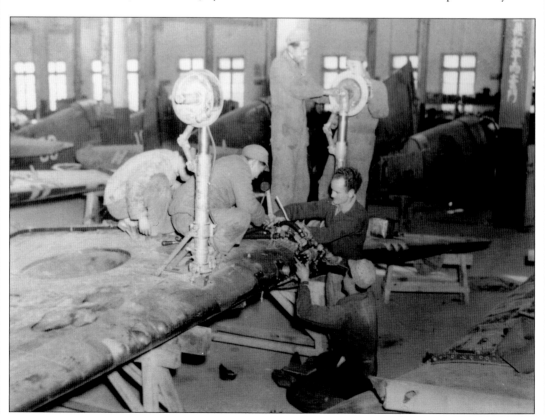

at last go home. They enjoyed the loose organisation of the AVG and did not look forward to the possibility of having to bend to spit-and-polish Army rules.

When the Tenth Air Force sent an induction team from India to pressure the AVG to sign up, the pilots wanted no part of it, and most of the groundcrew felt the same. Some resigned from the AVG immediately. The rest resolved to serve out their contracts, but would call it quits on Independence Day. The USAAF could have what remained of their dwindling force of P-40s, but that was all.

While all this was going on, nine Army pilots who would later serve in the 23rd FG arrived in China in May to gain combat experience flying with the AVG. One of these men was Maj Bruce K Holloway, a lanky West Pointer from Tennessee who wangled his way out of a staff job in Tenth Air Force headquarters by securing orders to report to Chennault as an observer of the AVG. He recorded his first impression of Chennault, who had just been promoted to brigadier general, in his diary;

'He is a sincere, interesting and affable man – none of the usual overbearing and obnoxious traits associated with some general officers in the US Army.'

Holloway flew several times with the AVG but did not see any action prior to joining the 23rd FG. He would see plenty after that, however. When he finally left China in the autumn of 1943, Holloway was both the group commander and the leading ace in the CBI with 13 confirmed victories. The lessons learned from Chennault continued to serve Holloway well throughout his military career, and he eventually retired from the USAF as a four-star general.

Fellow early arrival Capt Albert J 'Ajax' Baumler was the only one of the nine pilots with combat experience, having flown Polikarpov I-15 and I-16 fighters with the Republican forces in 1936-37 during the Spanish Civil War – he had claimed 4.5 kills and two probables during this period. Baumler flew with the US Army from 1938 to 1941, and then resigned his commission to join the AVG. His first attempt to reach China was cut

AVG armourers bore-site the guns of a newly arrived P-40E at Kunming in the spring of 1942. The AVG received about 30 E-models as attrition replacements for the Hawk 81-A2s acquired in 1941, and 18 of these survived long enough to be turned over to the 23rd FG. Some 28 of the 100 Tomahawks issued to the AVG were also handed over to the group when the former disbanded on 4 July 1942 (*AVG Association*)

CURTISS P-40 WARHAWK

The P-40 Warhawk, with a fearsome sharksmouth painted on its distinctive engine cowling, is one of the enduring images of World War 2. It was a handsome machine, with its pointed snout, tapered wings and voluptuously rounded tail surfaces. In photographs, paintings and even cartoons, the P-40 (or 'Shark' in 23rd FG parlance) came to symbolise America's war effort – tough, cocky and colourful.

The P-40 design had its roots in the earlier blunt-nosed Curtiss H-75 Hawk fighter, which was powered by a radial engines. Designed in 1934-35, the aircraft entered service with the USAAC in 1938 as the P-36. In an attempt to build a faster fighter, Curtiss proposed replacing the P-36's radial engine with the new Allison V-1710 liquid-cooled powerplant to create the P-40. The Army liked the idea – especially the fact that Curtiss would be able to produce the new aeroplane quickly – and it issued a contract for more than 500 of the fighters.

The P-40 did achieve an increase in top speed of nearly 50 mph over the P-36, but the new aeroplane suffered in other ways. Its greater weight slowed the rate of climb and reduced manoeuvrability compared to the P-36. Perhaps most importantly, the Allison engine produced maximum performance at an altitude of just 15,000 ft, which was far below the operational ceilings of contemporary European and Japanese fighters. This was not the fault of the engine so much as it was the product of outdated thinking on the part of the Army, which still saw fighters as medium-altitude, short-ranged weapons at that time.

Despite its shortcomings, the P-40 began to arrive at Army fighter bases in May 1940. Pilots found it tricky to take off and land in the aeroplane until they became accustomed to the high torque of its engine and the narrow track of its landing gear. Once in the air, they were most impressed by one aspect of the P-40's performance – its spectacular diving speed.

During 1940, Curtiss redesigned its P-40B/C to take advantage of the newly developed, more powerful, version of the Allison engine, the V-1710-39. The aircraft, designated H-87 by its manufacturer, had a new fuselage design with a lower thrust line and a bigger cockpit opening, and all of its guns were mounted in the wings. The British called the new aeroplane the Kittyhawk (the previous model had been dubbed the Tomahawk), and in US service it was known informally as the Warhawk. Starting with the P-40D, all future models – and they would be numerous – were modifications of the original H-87 design.

The P-40 was never the best performing fighter in the sky, but it was reliable, it carried heavy armament, and it could withstand amazing amounts of battle damage and still bring its pilot home safely. By the time production ended in 1944, Curtiss had built more than 15,000 P-40s of all types. They flew for more Allied nations than any other combat aircraft of World War 2.

Maj Bruce Holloway flies a 76th FS P-40E near Kunming in 1942. The plane lacks the *U.S. ARMY* marking under its wings, indicating that it may be one of the AVG hand-me-downs. The blue 76th FS fuselage band is barely visible (*Bill Johnson*)

short by the Pearl Harbor attack, so he rejoined the Army, but he soon wangled an assignment to China. Baumler finally arrived at Chennault's headquarters in Kunming in May 1942, and the following month found him at the AVG's easternmost base, Hengyang, itching for action. He soon got it.

As AVG engagements go, the air battle near Hengyang on 22 June was successful, but not extraordinary. At 1320 hrs, the Chinese warning net reported a force of 14 Japanese Ki-27 'Nate' fighters bearing down on Hengyang. AVG 2nd PS Vice Squadron Leader Ed Rector made a call for help to the 1st PS, based at nearby Kweilin, and then pulled together a flight of six P-40E Warhawks, including one flown by Baumler, to scramble against the incoming enemy force. Bad weather prevented P-40s at Kweilin from reaching Hengyang to join the fight, so Rector and his men had to go it alone.

A detailed record of the fight does not survive, but four Japanese fighters were claimed as destroyed for no losses. The citation for Baumler's first Air Medal credits him with one Ki-27 'Nate' destroyed that day. This gave Baumler the distinction of having scored the USAAF's first confirmed victory in the CBI Theatre. He would duly achieve an impressive record as a fighter pilot and squadron commander in China during the tumultuous year ahead.

While the AVG was holding the line in China, other Americans were busy ferrying P-40E fighters across Africa toward Karachi. These pilots already had one adventure behind them, having flown 68 aeroplanes off the deck of the aircraft carrier USS *Ranger* on 10 May to begin their journey. Their successful launch was no small feat, because the P-40 – a heavy aircraft with a slow rate of climb – had not been designed with the take-off capabilities needed for carrier operations. Eventually, 25 of these pilots would be assigned to the 23rd FG, the rest filling out the ranks of the 51st FG, which had recently arrived in India with just a handful of P-40s.

Life went on as before for the 23rd FG at New Malir until 12 June, when orders arrived to send a detail of 19 enlisted men to Kunming, site of the AVG's headquarters. By this time it was known that the 23rd would be taking over from the AVG on 4 July, but it still was not clear how. To complicate matters, Maj Culbertson fell ill at New Malir and was hospitalised, while the group adjutant, Maj Peter Borre, was reassigned to the air base command at Karachi. Now the 23rd FG could add a lack of leadership to its long list of other obvious shortcomings.

Repair facilities, such as the No 10 Factory in Kunming, helped to keep the 23rd FG supplied with aircraft by rebuilding damaged aeroplanes and stripping parts from others that were beyond repair. Seen here in 1942, the factory is working on four P-40s plus a Republic P-43A at bottom left. Note the Chinese insignia on the P-40 wing in the foreground (*Don Hyatt*)

The group's advance detachment arrived at Kunming on 15 June, and the men were pleasantly surprised by their new duty station. In the foothills of the Himalayas at an altitude of 6230 ft, Kunming had a cool climate that was a welcome relief from the June heat of India. The airfield sat at the northern end of Tien Chih Lake (also called Lake Kunming) and featured a crushed-stone runway that was 6137 ft long and 375 ft wide running northeast to southwest so as to take advantage of the prevailing winds. The city of Kunming itself, situated about three miles north of the airfield, was packed with refugees who had fled from Japanese-occupied areas of China.

The men, under the direction of AVG Squadron Leader Arvid Olson, began working alongside AVG groundcrews in their specialities to learn their jobs as quickly as possible. More USAAF personnel arrived in the days that followed and pitched in immediately. On 18 June the first USAAF pilots arrived in Kunming to begin training on the AVG P-40s that would be turned over to them in a few weeks. By this time the AVG was down to just 48 operational fighters – a mixture of early model P-40Bs (Curtiss designation Hawk 81-A2) and the remains of 35 P-40Es that began arriving as replacements in late March. Obviously, the latter aircraft had logged fewer hours than the older P-40s, but all had seen heavy service in the AVG.

NEW COMMANDING OFFICER

When Chennault learned that the ailing Culbertson would not be coming with the 23rd FG to China, he had to scramble to find a new CO to lead the group. The command structure called for an officer with the rank of

Col Robert L Scott, seen here in the cockpit of a P-40E, commanded the 23rd FG from mid-July 1942 until early January 1943. He returned to the US as the leading ace in China with ten confirmed victories, and went on to write the best-selling book about his experiences in the CBI, *God Is My Co-Pilot* (*Bill Johnson*)

One of just five AVG pilots who accepted induction into the USAAF and stayed on with the 23rd FG was Maj Wesley Sawyer, who flew in the 76th FS until December 1942. He scored two victories with the AVG and one more in August 1942 with the 76th FS (*Dwayne Tabatt*)

lieutenant colonel or full colonel, and Chennault knew he needed someone with fighter experience and an aggressive nature. Fortunately, he knew where to find just such a man.

Col Robert L Scott was a 34-year-old West Point graduate who had spent most of his pre-war career flying fighters, but at this moment was cooling his heels in the Assam-Burma-China Ferry Command, flying transports from Dinjan, in India, across the 'Hump' into China. In his spare time, Scott used a P-40E borrowed from the AVG to fly patrols out of Dinjan over the western portion of the 'Hump' route. Scott got his new assignment to the 23rd FG on 20 June and flew up to Kunming a week later to begin organising his headquarters.

Meanwhile, 4 July and the dissolution of the AVG were moving inexorably closer. Chennault took stock of the situation and realised that the 23rd FG could not possibly be ready to take over by that date. He sat down for heart-to-heart talks with some of his most trusted AVG pilots and eventually convinced five of them to stay on with him and accept commissions in the USAAF. These men – Majs Frank Schiel, David L 'Tex' Hill, Edward F Rector, J Gilpin 'Gil' Bright and Capt Charles W Sawyer – would give the new squadrons of the 23rd FG a hard core of combat experience that would help to carry them through the difficult first five months in combat in China.

In addition, 18 AVG pilots agreed to delay their departure for two weeks following 4 July, providing Chennault with just enough flyers to hold the line until additional USAAF pilots arrived. Just as important, 33 AVG ground personnel agreed to be inducted into the Army and stay on in China with the 23rd FG. Their technical skills and experience would be of inestimable value in the months ahead.

The 23rd FG suffered its first casualty since arriving in China on the morning of 3 July 1942. Pvt Marshall F F Brown was servicing the wing guns of a P-40 at Kunming when another enlisted man working in the cockpit accidentally tripped the trigger on the aeroplane's control column. Brown was standing directly in front of the fighter's two 0.30-cal wing guns when they fired a short burst. Two rounds struck the private in the head, killing him instantly. Brown was buried in the local cemetery two days later.

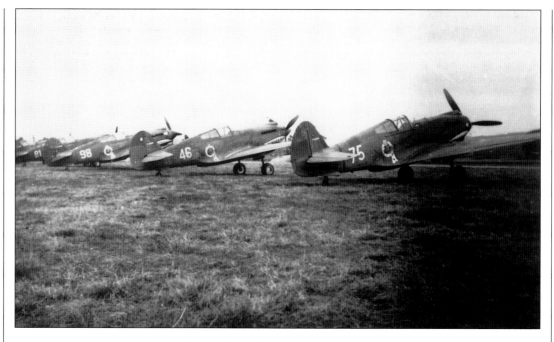

Former 3rd PS AVG Tomahawks, now assigned to the 74th FS/ 23rd FG, are parked at Kunming in the summer of 1942. Although these aircraft still carry their CAF serial numbers on their rudders, they also display the 23rd FG badge. Although not visible in this photograph, the Chinese national insignias on the wings have been replaced with the US star-on-disc (*Leon Klesman*)

Madame Chiang Kai-shek, the wife of China's leader and titular head of the CAF, hosted a farewell party for the few remaining AVG members in Chungking (now Chongqing) before they went home, but there was no other event to mark the group's passing into history. Likewise, there was no ceremony at Kunming on 4 July 1942 for the official activation of the 23rd FG and its three squadrons. A formation of P-40s went up and made several low passes over the airfield for the benefit of the press photographers on hand, but that was it. After all, there was a war on.

In fact, the P-40s at Hengyang fought the AVG's very last engagement that same day, the pilots involved claiming four confirmed victories against Ki-27 'Nates' that were attempting to perform a strafing attack on the airfield.

GROUP DISPERSES

On 5 July, 'Tex' Hill led a flight of nine P-40s from Kunming to Kweilin (now Guilin), where he would assume command of the 75th FS. The squadron was to be based at Hengyang, and there to fly with Hill were 'Gil' Bright, 'Ajax' Baumler, four USAAF lieutenants and a handful of AVG pilots. That same day, Ed Rector and Charlie Sawyer flew from Hengyang to Kweilin, where their 76th FS would be based. They had an even smaller Army contingent of just three lieutenants, plus some more AVG pilots.

Frank Schiel had a different assignment with the 74th FS. He had a full complement of 18 Army lieutenants at Kunming, but none of them had been in China more than a few days. As commander of the 'School Squadron', it would fall on Schiel to train these pilots in how to fight Chennault-style, whilst at the same time providing air defence for Kunming. The 74th took over the red-banded aircraft of the 3rd PS, the 75th got the 1st PS's P-40s with their white squadron markings, while the 76th took on the blue squadron colour of the 2nd PS.

Pilots of the 16th FS attempt to relax in the open-air alert shack at Peishiyi shortly after arriving in China in July 1942. The 16th FS/51st FG was attached to the 23rd FG to provide air defence for the Chinese capital at Chungking, but it soon moved to the eastern China front (*George Barnes*)

Rounding out Chennault's fighter force was the 16th FS, attached for service from the 51st FG in India. This squadron was supposedly 'loaned' to Chennault for the air defence of Chungking, but its assignment there only lasted a few days. Under the command of Maj Harry B Young, the 16th FS would move east on 12 July to Lingling, midway between Hengyang and Kweilin. Its P-40E-1s were easily distinguishable from the aeroplanes of the other three squadrons because they were the only ones displaying the American national insignia – a white star on a dark blue disc – on their fuselages. The 16th, officially still a unit of the 51st FG, used numbers 11 to 39 to identify its P-40s.

The only other USAAF combat aircraft in China at that time were a handful of B-25 Mitchell twin-engined bombers assigned to the 11th Bomb Squadron (BS) at Kunming.

It would fall on the shoulders of 'Tex' Hill, based farthest east at Hengyang, to lead the bulk of the 23rd FG's missions during its first few weeks of operations. Already an ace with 11 confirmed victories, Hill was

The old and the new mingle on the 75th FS flightline at Chanyi. The Tomahawk in the foreground carries the 23rd FG badge and the 75th FS white stripe on its fuselage, but no aircraft number. Next in line are two brand new P-40E-1s or Ks, and then a P-40E. (*James L Lee*)

a big man at 6 ft 2 in tall. With his slow drawl, colourful language and gifts as a storyteller, he was a natural leader. Hill recalled those early days in the 23rd FG;

'The 23rd was unique in that it was formed in the field under combat conditions. For instance, in my case I was a squadron leader in the AVG. I came down off a flight and they said, 'Take the oath and sign here. You're now Maj Hill, 75th Fighter Squadron'. Chennault's directions were very, very simple. He said, 'Just try to kill every damned Jap you can find any way you can'. As American people, being very resourceful, we dreamed up all kinds of ways to do things.

'We were pretty much on our own. Our squadrons were all separated, especially in the early days. Later on they got better organised. What we would do is move up into these advanced bases (such as Hengyang). All we'd have is fuel, bombs and ammo. Of course the Japs would know the minute we got there, and they'd be there the next morning. We'd fight out of those bases until we'd lose our combat effectiveness, then we'd move back to the rear echelon and regroup. If we could have sustained our positions, I believe we could have attrited the Japanese Army Air Force (JAAF) from our China bases.'

In mid-morning on 6 July 1942, Hill took off from Kweilin, leading a flight of four P-40s that were assigned to escort five B-25s of the 11th BS on a mission to bomb installations at Canton (now Guangzhou). The tiny formation climbed through a low overcast and headed south towards the target. Fortunately, the clouds broke up over Canton, allowing the B-25s to make their run over the target at 5000 ft and score direct hits on several warehouses along the Pearl River, before turning for home. Thirty miles out of Canton, one of the B-25 pilots radioed that he was under attack.

Hill checked the sky around him to make sure that there were no other enemy fighters lurking in the clouds, prior to leading his flight in a diving attack on the Ki-27s. He had little trouble picking out one of the 'Nates'

A pilot stands next to a 16th FS P-40E-1 at Kweilin. Note the heavy exhaust staining on the fuselage. In early September 1942, 23rd FG commander Col Scott complained in a memo that the P-40s flown by the 16th FS were worn out, having served as trainers in the US before coming to China (*George Barnes*)

and hitting it with a telling burst of 0.50-cal 'slugs'. The fighter caught fire and dove into the ground. Meanwhile, AVG pilot John Petach, leading the second element, engaged three more Ki-27s. He filed this report;

'All three started to turn towards me. I opened fire at 500 yards but was shooting behind the last man, so I pulled the nose of my aeroplane well ahead of the enemy aircraft and gave him a one-second burst. Then the enemy aircraft pulled into sight right in front of my nose so that my fire raked him as he passed. I saw large holes in his wings, but the other two aeroplanes started to make a pass at me so I pulled up and took off. I pulled away and saw two more about three miles north of our combat. I turned toward them, and this time they turned away and headed for a mountain. The first aeroplane was just turning around the mountain top when I overhauled the second fighter. I gave him about a one-second burst, and he erupted in flame and was burning well when Hill called all aeroplanes from combat. At that point I broke off my attack and joined up.'

Hill and Petach were each credited with one Ki-27 destroyed, and Petach also claimed a probable during the course of the 23rd FG's first offensive mission. Sadly he was killed four days later while leading a dive-bombing attack on the town of Linchuan, which the Japanese were holding against Chinese ground forces. Fellow AVG pilot Arnold Shamblin was also lost on the mission. He reportedly baled out and was captured by the Japanese, but he did not survive his imprisonment.

On 19 July, the last of the AVG pilots boarded transport aeroplanes at Kunming to begin their long journey home. By that time, more USAAF pilots had arrived to fill out the ranks of the 75th and 76th FSs. Rector's 76th crew at Kweilin, for example, now consisted of 13 pilots including himself and Sawyer. Ready or not, they would have to take the fight to the Japanese in China from here.

Ex-AVG Tomahawk '49' undergoes outdoor repairs, probably at Kunming. Note the different camouflage colours visible where the wing fairing has been removed. Also, a small turtle has been painted behind the shoulder of the flying tiger (*Don Hyatt*)

CHINA AIR TASK FORCE

Brig Gen Claire L Chennault was appointed commanding officer of the China Air Task Force (CATF) as part of the Tenth Air Force in China on 24 June 1942. He was 49 years old, in only fair health, and nearly exhausted after five years of fighting the Japanese in China. The CATF was a tiny force consisting of the four P-40 squadrons and the 11th BS (Medium) with B-25s.

Initially numbering just 70 aircraft, the CATF faced a formidable assignment. The Japanese flanked Chiang Kai-shek's Free China on the east, south and west. To the north was the USSR, which maintained neutrality with Japan. The loss of Burma in the spring had severed China's last supply link to the outside world. Nothing could move in or out of China by road, rail or ship. The only avenue left was the air. Following the fall of Rangoon, transport aircraft began plying the hazardous 450-mile route from Chabua and Dinjan, in India's remote Assam Valley, over the rugged Himalayan Mountains to Kunming. They brought everything from ammunition and gasoline to toothpaste and toilet paper for the fighting forces in China via this route, which soon became known worldwide as the 'Hump'.

It was absolutely vital to keep the 'Hump' supply line open, so the CATF's top priority was to protect its transport aircraft and its eastern

Civilian and military transport aircraft, including this USAAF C-47, plied the 'Hump' route between India and Kunming daily to deliver supplies that were essential in keeping China in the war. The 23rd FG provided cover for the China end of the air corridor during 1942-43 (*Mrs G H Steidle*)

terminus at Kunming from enemy air attacks. In addition, the CATF was expected to provide air support for Chinese ground forces facing the Japanese along the border with Burma and in central China.

To further complicate the CATF's mission, the Japanese maintained airfields in a ring around Free China, from the Hankow (now Wuhan) area northeast of Hengyang to Canton and Hong Kong on the coast, and Hainan Island in the South China Sea to Hanoi, in French Indochina (now Vietnam). Fortunately for the CATF, the JAAF never had enough combat aircraft in China to operate from all of these bases at once, however, although it moved its units frequently, and could strike Chinese targets from any direction at any time.

The location and quality of the CATF airfields in China worked to its advantage. Like the warning net, Chennault's network of bases was a constant work in progress. Kunming, in Yunnan Province, served not only as the point of entry for 'Hump' flights arriving in China, but also as the headquarters for Chennault and the CATF. From Kunming, it was roughly 300 miles southwest to Lashio (the most advanced enemy air base in Burma), 330 miles south to Hanoi and 380 miles north to Chungking, Chiang Kai-shek's capital city.

Flying eastward from Kunming to the CATF's other primary bases, it was 425 miles to Kweilin, 105 miles farther to Lingling and 65 miles beyond there to Hengyang. From these three sites, the CATF could strike at the Japanese in Canton and Hong Kong on the coast, and up north in the Hankow area. Literally dozens of other airfields were either available for Chennault's use or were under construction. Several of these were located behind Japanese lines in unoccupied areas controlled by Chinese guerrilla forces.

Virtually all of the airfields in China featured runways built by hand out of crushed gravel. Although they were not as smooth as paved surfaces,

Airfields in China featured crushed rock runways, built by hand. Here, a team of Chinese workers pulls a heavy roller over the Kweilin runway, while a C-47 lands in the background. The gravel runways were hard on tyres, but bomb craters were easily repaired (*Tom Raleigh*)

and were therefore hard on aircraft tyres, crushed gravel runways were nearly impossible to destroy. A direct hit by an enemy bomb might gouge a hole in the surface, but within minutes a huge crew of Chinese workers would descend on the damaged area with picks and shovels, wheelbarrows and hand-drawn rollers. The runway could be back in service by the time the Japanese bombers had returned to base.

NIGHTFIGHTING

During the early weeks in the 23rd FG's history, the Japanese had established a pattern of sending small formations of bombers over the east China bases at night on harassment missions. At Lingling, the 16th FS pilots took the abuse for as long as they could, but on the night of 26-27 July two of them decided to fight back when three bombers were reported approaching the field. Capt Ed Goss and 1Lt John 'Moe' Lombard, who were both future aces, scrambled in their P-40s at around 0100 hrs. Goss got off first and managed to spot the bombers, which were flying with their formation lights on. He made three passes at them over the field, possibly damaging one of the bombers, before they turned off their lights and disappeared into the night. Lombard did not make contact.

Later that night Goss scrambled again, this time with another future ace, 1Lt Dallas Clinger, on his wing. The enemy bombers turned back before reaching Lingling, and the P-40 pilots returned to base disappointed.

Word of the attempted night interceptions quickly spread throughout the 23rd FG. At Hengyang, Capts John Alison and 'Ajax' Baumler of the 75th FS sat down to work out plans for a successful night interception. Their chance to try out their theories came on the night of 29-30 July. On the report of incoming raiders, the pair took off at about 0200 hrs. Alison got away first, passing through a thin layer of haze at 9000 ft. Upon reaching an altitude of 12,000 ft, he commenced circling, his eyes straining in the darkness to pick out the approaching enemy bombers (possibly Mitsubishi Ki-21 'Sallys', identified as Type 97s by the USAAF pilots involved). Soon Alison's radio crackled with the message that enemy bombers had just passed over Hengyang from north to south without attacking. The next message said that the enemy aircraft had turned onto a reciprocal course and were heading back in the direction of the airfield.

Alison assumed that he had missed spotting the bombers because they had passed below the haze layer, but then he had another thought – perhaps they were above him. As he flew over the field he looked up to his left and saw shadows passing against the stars, along with the telltale glow of the bombers' exhaust flames. Alison pulled his P-40 into a climb and called in his sighting to Baumler, who was close by.

As Alison reached 15,000 ft and drew level with his quarry, the twin-engined bombers banked to the right and made a 180-degree turn that would position them for a third run over the field. Apparently, the turn placed Alison's P-40 between one of the bombers and the moon, because the tail gunner in the aeroplane to Alison's right opened fire. A stream of tracers caught the P-40 in the nose and stitched it down the length of the fuselage. Alison, not knowing how badly his fighter was damaged, immediately started shooting at the bomber directly in front of him.

A two-second burst from his six 0.50-cal guns ripped into the bomber, and it fell away from the formation. Then Alison turned his guns on the bomber to his right that had damaged his P-40. He fired again, and this time his target burst into flames and fell in pieces from the sky. Men on the field at Hengyang saw the exchange of fire and then watched the falling fireball. By now the engine in Alison's P-40 had begun to smoke, and it was throwing oil back over the fighter's windscreen.

When Alison launched his attack, Baumler was still several thousand feet below and climbing for all he was worth. He saw Alison's first victim fall away from the other two and decided his best course of action would be to finish off the damaged machine. After a short chase, he pulled into firing position behind the bomber and cut loose. The latter staggered as it erupted in flames, before diving into the ground. At this point a gunner in yet another bomber opened fire on Baumler, alerting him to its presence. He chased this aeroplane for about 30 miles before catching up with it and blowing it out of the sky.

Meanwhile, Alison continued to fight, although the engine in his P-40 was by now running very roughly. Maintaining visual contact with the third bomber in the original group that he had spotted, Alison reached firing range just after the aeroplane had dropped its bombs. In the final few seconds before his engine died, Alison got off three bursts, the third of which must have directly hit the bomber's fuel tanks because the aeroplane literally exploded.

At almost the same moment, the engine in Alison's P-40 gasped and quit. He opened the canopy to improve his vision and turned to attempt a dead-stick landing at Hengyang. Just as he began his approach, flames belched out from under the engine cowling, momentarily stunning and distracting Alison, who in turn overshot the airfield. In the final few seconds of flight, he nursed the P-40 over some buildings and trees, then set it down on the surface of the Hsiang River.

Three war-weary P-40Es that saw combat in China with the 23rd FG during 1942 sit on the ramp at Landhi Field near Karachi, in India, where they are in service with an operational training unit. '12' (left) and '37' came from the 16th FS, while '100' had previously served with the 76th FS (*George Aldridge*)

The Japanese fighter most often encountered by the 23rd FG was the Nakajima Ki-43 Hayabusa (Allied code name 'Oscar'). This captured example was repainted in Chinese markings at Kweilin. Pilots of the 23rd FG often misidentified the Ki-43 as a 'Zero', especially early on in the war (*Everett Hyatt*)

Now it was Baumler's turn to land, but the field at Hengyang remained blacked out. Two members of the 75th FS rushed to set out a line of lanterns down each side of the runway, thus giving Baumler the light he needed to land safely. Alison and Baumler were each awarded two confirmed victories for the mission, and both pilots were later decorated for their bravery.

Baumler was in action again within hours when the Japanese sent a mixed force of about 30 fighters (Ki-27 'Nates' and new Ki-43 'Oscars') back to Hengyang. 'Tex' Hill, 'Gil' Bright and Baumler led a group of P-40s from the 75th and 16th FSs in an attack at 19,000 ft not far from the field. Hill made a head-on pass at a Ki-27, which was critically damaged by the P-40 pilot's accurate burst of fire. With no hope of making it home, the JAAF pilot nosed over and aimed his stricken machine at a dummy P-40 that had been parked on the airfield at Hengyang. The death dive missed the 'fighter' by about 50 ft, with the 'Nate' burying itself in the ground near the end of the runway.

The air battle raged for about 15 minutes. Bright put a burst into a Ki-43 from behind and saw the aircraft nose over before he had to take evasive action to shake off another 'Oscar' that was approaching from his rear. Using his superior speed, Bright made a shallow climb and pulled away from the attacker. As this was happening, Bright's wingman followed the first 'Oscar' down and repeatedly hit it prior to the Japanese fighter crashing.

Now Bright headed back into the dogfight and attempted to get onto the tail of another Ki-27. The 'Nate' pilot spotted the approaching P-40 and snap-turned so tightly that he was now in a position to make a head-on pass at Bright's Warhawk. Unperturbed, Bright took aim and the 'Nate' was struck a series of telling blows by the P-40's heavy calibre

0.50-cal machine guns. The Japanese fighter pulled up sharply before dropping off in a spin, trailing white smoke. Bright could not stick around to watch the Ki-27 crash, however, because he had to evade yet another enemy fighter attempting to attack him.

Hill, Bright and Baumler were each credited with one victory, and future ace 1Lt Bob Liles of the 16th FS got a probable for his squadron's first claim.

Enemy fighters came back to Hengyang again early the next morning (31 July). This time, separate P-40 flights from the 75th and 16th met them, and yet another one-sided battle erupted. Three future aces of the 16th – Goss, Clinger and Lombard – claimed their first victories in the fight, and a further three kills were credited to Maj Bright, 1Lt Henry Elias and 2Lt Mack Mitchell of the 75th. Later that morning, Col Scott claimed two victories near Leiyang while flying by himself. In the past 31 hours, the pilots of the 23rd FG had tallied 15 confirmed victories for the cost of just one P-40. Chennault's new boys had met the challenge and were ready for more. This fact was not lost on the Chinese.

Civilian and military leaders at Lingling expressed their gratitude to the 16th FS on 1 August by presenting the squadron with a large blue-and-white banner proclaiming it 'The Great Wall of the Air'. This banner, on which the Great Wall of China was portrayed with a shark's mouth and small yellow wings, became the inspiration for the 16th's squadron badge. Later, this emblem was painted on the fuselages of most of the unit's P-40s. Similar ceremonies took place in Hengyang to honour the pilots and groundcrews stationed there.

More action followed, but it was not until 8 August that the 76th FS at last managed to score its first victories. On that day, Charlie Sawyer led a four-aeroplane flight out of Kweilin, escorting B-25s to attack White Cloud

2Lt Dallas A Clinger scored the 16th FS's first victory on 31 July 1942 at Hengyang, and he went on to become a five-victory ace. His adventurous spirit is amply on display in this photograph, as he puts a motorcycle through its paces at Karachi prior to his transfer to China (*Jack Best*)

airfield at Canton. The following extract from the 76th FS's official unit history described the fight, which began at 1136 hrs;

'As the bombers hit their objective, Lt (Patrick) Daniels peeled off and attacked a flight of three Zeros. He spun out of the turn in his first attack, but recovered with three Zeros on his tail. However, he managed to pull away from them with full throttle. Two of the Zeros fell far behind and turned back, but the third Zero followed. Lt Daniels made a quick turn and a head-on run with the Jap. The Zero pilot pulled up to escape the gunfire of the P-40, and to gain position where he could fire on Daniels' canopy from above. Daniels pulled up tightly and saw his tracers from his six 0.50-cals go through the Zero just as the Jap was about to fire at him. The Zero caught fire and Lt Daniels saw the pilot crawl back on the fuselage of the aeroplane just before it crashed on top of a mountain.

'As the bombers started homeward, Capt Sawyer saw a flight of nine Zeros and I-97s (almost certainly Ki-43s and Ki-27s) coming up to intercept the bombers. He peeled off and headed for the flight. Lt (Charles) DuBois, thinking the flight leader was going down to strafe the aerodrome as planned, followed the captain. In the engagement that followed, Capt Sawyer shot down one I-97. Both Capt Sawyer's and Lt Daniels' victories were confirmed.'

Further victories were claimed on 11 and 17 August, but then the reality of war in China set in. Supplies of ammunition and gasoline were running low, the weather was turning sour, the P-40s needed servicing and the pilots and groundcrews were getting fatigued. Chennault made the decision to pull his squadrons out of east China for the time being. The 16th FS returned to Peishiyi, the 76th joined the 74th at Kunming and the 75th went to the new base at Chanyi (now Zhanyi), 50 miles northeast of Kunming.

Japanese commanders opposing the CATF used high-flying reconnaissance aircraft – primarily twin-engined Ki-46 'Dinahs' – to try to keep track of Chennault's mobile forces. The 74th FS 'School Squadron' at Kunming got its first taste of combat on 8 September 1942 when a single P-40 was sent up to try to intercept one of the snoopers. Maj Bruce K

B-25s of the 11th BS taxi out for a mission in the autumn of 1942. The 23rd FG squadrons often provided fighter escorts for the 11th BS, which was the only other combat unit assigned to the CATF. Note the dusty field conditions (*Doug Erickson*)

Sgts Cotton and Orwin attempt to raise 74th FS Tomahawk '59', which was apparently taxied into a ditch at Kunming. This ex-AVG fighter gave the 74th FS so much trouble that it was eventually nicknamed the 'Yunnan Whore'! (*Leon Klesman*)

Holloway, who was serving as 23rd FG operations officer at the time, described the action in his diary. This entry also provides a look at the CATF's employment of the warning net;

'Started getting plots of one enemy ship around Paoshan at about 0845 hrs, then another of one aeroplane coming this way from the direction of Hanoi. Regular plots of this aeroplane came up to the 200-km circle and then we got no more. At this point, I sent up P-40B "46", piloted by Lt Thomas R Smith, and gave him instructions to go as high as he could and circle the field. Heard nothing more until about 1000 hrs, when Iliang (only 30 km away) reported a dogfight going on overhead. I immediately sent out Lt Daniels in P-40E "104" to give aid.

'There were no details given of the dogfight whatever over the Chinese net – not even the number of aeroplanes involved. However, I considered there was only one enemy aeroplane since it had been pretty definitely one on the plots coming up – therefore, I did not alert the command other than putting all pursuit units on station.

'Well, Smith shot him down – a twin-engined I-45 (Ki-46). It was a great day for the 74th, with much rejoicing – good for its heretofore rather low state of morale. Smith did one victory roll over the field very low (indication of one aeroplane shot down) and made a very short circuit before landing. He was so excited, however, that he overshot the field and had to go around again.

'The first blood for the 74th FS, which has been sitting here for two months and not even seen an enemy aeroplane.'

Smith reported that he had caught the JAAF aeroplane at 24,000 ft and pulled in close behind it. He put one burst into its left engine and then five into the right engine, which caught fire. He was so close behind the damaged enemy aeroplane that it sprayed oil all over the leading edges of his wings and tail surfaces. Finally, the stricken machine nosed over into a long dive and crashed into the ground. It was Smith's only confirmed victory of the war, and three months later he was decorated with a Silver Star for the action.

REACHING OUT

Chennault would shuttle his P-40s in and out of the eastern bases throughout the rest of 1942. Deploying in squadron and even down to flight strength, pilots would show up at Hengyang, Lingling or Kweilin on short notice, fly a couple of missions, and then pull out again for the relative safety of the Kunming area. At the same time, Chennault began to look south into French Indochina and west into northern Burma for more targets to attack.

On 25 September, the CATF struck Hanoi in force for the first time when nine P-40s, led by Maj Ed Rector of the 76th FS at Kunming, escorted four B-25s in an attack on Gia Lam airfield. The fighters stopped at an auxiliary airfield near the Chinese border at Mengtze to top off with fuel so that they could then return to Kunming non-stop. Rector led the close escort, with Col Bob Scott leading the top cover.

A flight of 13 twin-engined Japanese fighters, possibly new Ki-45 'Nicks', were waiting as the Americans approached the target, and they attempted to attack the B-25s. Rector's flight of four was able to cut them off, and a swirling dogfight ensued. Rector shot down two, and the other three members of his flight – 2Lts Pat Daniels, Tim Marks and Howard Krippner – each got one apiece.

After the B-25s had turned for home, Col Scott spotted a flight of three enemy fighters climbing toward the retreating bombers. Intercepting them, Scott claimed to have shot up all three aircraft, and he was duly credited with one confirmed victory and a probable. This kill was his fifth, which made him the first USAAF pilot to attain ace status in the 23rd FG.

Officers of the 76th FS gather at Kunming in mid-September 1942. Sat in the bottom row are, from left to right, Patrick Daniels (KIA), Charles DuBois, Howard Krippner (KIA), Gordon Kitzman, Bruce Smith (adjutant) and Edward Rector (commanding officer). Second row, from left to right, are Jasper Harrington (engineering chief), Harold Stuart, C W Sawyer, Edward Dangrove (flight surgeon), unknown, M D 'Tim' Marks and Arthur Waite. Top row, from left to right, are unknown and Jewell Matthews (*Bill Johnson*)

By the time the war ended, 40 more pilots would join him on the 23rd FG's roster of aces.

25 September was also the day that the CATF reported the arrival of 20 new fighter pilots at Kunming. This was the first significant influx of pilots since the formation of the 23rd FG some three months previous. Even more important, these new aviators had been seasoned during long months of patrol and training duties in the Panama Canal Zone. They knew how to fly, and they knew how to shoot. Very quickly, they learned how to fight Chennault-style as well. More good pilots would follow from Panama in coming months.

The CATF next turned its attention to an even bigger target – the famous port city of Hong Kong. This first mission, a long-planned strike against the docks at Kowloon, was flown on 25 October, with seven P-40s of the 75th and 76th FSs escorting 12 B-25s. Chennault shuttled his attack force into Kweilin early that morning, and the mission to Hong Kong, some 325 miles away, took off at 1130 hrs. The 75th FS unit history gave this description of the mission;

Studebaker fuel truck No 119 refuels a line of new 76th FS P-40Ks at Kunming in the autumn of 1942. The 23rd FG carried out numerous strafing and reconnaissance missions against traffic and installations along 'The Burma Road' during this period, before escorting B-25s to Hong Kong for the first time on 25 October (*Bill Johnson*)

The arrangement for the defence of China was simple – the US provided the airpower and the Chinese provided the manpower. Here, Chinese workers at Kunming carry a Allison V-1710 engine from a 23rd FG P-40 using age-old technology (*Leon Klesman*)

31

16th FS pilot Capt Clyde B Slocumb poses with his P-40E-1 – possibly No 16 (41-24927). Slocumb was credited with shooting down an enemy bomber on 2 November 1942. He returned to China for a second tour in 1944 as CO of the 75th FS, and assumed command of the 23rd FG after the war had ended (*Clyde Slocumb*)

'The bombers did some good work on the docks and headed for home when a few Zeros appeared. While the Japs were making up their minds on how to hit the bombers, the top cover picked off a few of the Zeros. Maj Hill took his flight into a formation of six Japs. He caught the first one, Col Scott got another, Capt Hampshire a third one and Lt Sher of the 76th the fourth. One of the Japs got on the tail of a B-25, and although he was fortunate enough to shoot down the first B-25 in this theatre, his good fortune was immediately followed by bad in the form of Capt Hampshire, who had heard the bomber's call for help and had 'sandwiched' the Jap, sending him spinning to earth less part of one wing.'

Capt John Hampshire and Lt Morton Sher were two of the new Panama pilots flying their first mission. Another new Panama pilot in the

Chinese soldiers relax in the alert shack at Hengyang while 75th FS pilot Capt John Hampshire catches up on his reading. Hampshire, one of the many fighter pilots who came to China in 1942 after service in the Panama Canal Zone, was the leading ace in China with 13 confirmed victories when he was killed in action on 2 May 1943 (*D J Klaasen*)

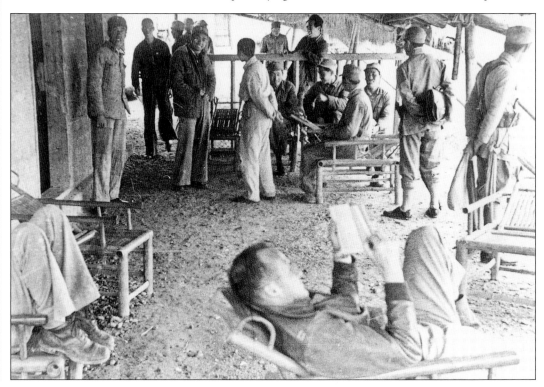

76th, 1Lt Charles DuBois, also saw his first action later that day when a flight of P-40s scrambled from Kunming to intercept a Japanese formation approaching from Indochina. The six P-40s met a mixed force of Ki-43 'Oscars' and Ki-45 'Nicks' near the border, 30 miles south of Mentze, and claimed four destroyed and four probables for no losses. DuBois claimed two of the victories, then scored a third kill two days later in a similar encounter over Mengtze.

The following month, the 23rd FG added three more pilots to its roster of aces in a single day. The mission was planned as a return to Hong Kong in force on 27 November, with ten B-25s escorted by 23 P-40s of the 16th, 74th and 75th FSs. The night before the strike, however, a strong wind blew up from the south. The headwind, combined with a shortage of 75-gallon drop tanks for the P-40s, forced the CATF to change its target to Canton. Japanese fighters were up in force to oppose the raiders, and a huge air battle quickly developed. The best description of the mission comes from the diary of Maj Holloway of the 76th, who led the top cover flight;

'We came into the target area from the north at 19,000 ft. When about 15 miles from the city, the bombers split into three flights – one to bomb the aircraft factory, the second to attack Tien Ho airfield and the third to target any shipping in the river. About the same time they split, Ed Goss (16th FS) ran into ten Zeros over to the left, and the fight was on. I didn't take my flight over there but stayed with the bombers until they reached their targets.

'I stayed with the ones who bombed a ship of about 8000 tons. They achieved several direct hits on the vessel and practically tore it to pieces. Right after this, another fight started under us – Alison got his flight into

New P-40Ks of the 75th FS get attention during refuelling on the flightline at Hengyang. The longer teeth at the front of the mouth were a trademark of the 75th FS 'Sharks'. The third fighter in the line carries the name *ROSE MARIE* in white below its exhaust stacks (*Bill Harris*)

this one, and by then the radio conversation was getting good. Everybody was yelling for someone else to shoot a Jap off his tail. I heard Clinger say to (1Lt Jack) Best, "I just knocked one off your tail, but you ought to move over. I almost hit you, too". About this time I saw a parachute descending directly ahead, and since the bombers seemed to be getting away all right, I went on to investigate the parachute, thinking it was from a silver-coloured aeroplane in the distance.

'By this time I was right over Tien Ho aerodrome, so I dived down into the fight. I was really going strong, and my flight pitched into the middle of it. I made a pass on a Zero and it burst into flames – I didn't see it hit the ground, as I had already started looking for others. They were all over the place, and you could see tracer bullets going in every direction. I saw burning Japanese aeroplanes falling all over the sky. I made several more runs on Zeros and I-97s and finally got into a good position on an I-97 and gave him a long burst. I don't know whether he went down or not – I claimed him as a probable.

'After this I climbed back to 8000 ft and barged in again. By this time I could see only about three Japs left milling around over the field like mosquitoes. All the P-40s had either left or were chasing some Jap out over the countryside. The three that were left were very elusive, and I didn't get a good pass at any of them. Finally, two of them got on my tail, so I left the vicinity in somewhat of a hurry and started for home. I could hear everybody talking about how many they shot down, and it certainly sounded good.

'I proceeded on toward home all by myself, looking around behind me all the time, when I saw an aeroplane off to my left going back toward Canton. It was a twin-engined light bomber and was very low over the hills. I turned in behind him and gave chase. Apparently he never did see me. I pulled on up to within about 100 yards behind him, expecting the rear gunner to open up on me at any instant. Either there was no rear gunner, or he was asleep. I opened up from directly astern and poured lead into him. The whole right side of the aeroplane burst into flames, and

Lt Sam Berman of the 76th FS poses in the cockpit of P-40K '103' in late 1942. Note the AVG-style tiger decal and the two-colour topside camouflage on the aircraft. Berman made a forced landing in Japanese-held territory in May 1943 but was rescued by Chinese guerrillas and returned to his squadron two weeks later (*Bill Johnson*)

Capt John D 'Moe' Lombard was the first ace of the 16th FS, scoring his fifth victory on 27 November 1942. He subsequently claimed two more kills and was promoted to commander of the 74th FS before being lost in bad weather in June 1943 (*Bruce Holloway*))

immediately thereafter there was an explosion that tore off the entire right wing. The flaming wreckage fell off to the left and crashed into the ground. It made a beautiful fire, and the whole thing took less time than it does to tell about it. I turned around and went home – I didn't have a single bullet hole in my aeroplane.'

When all the claims had been tallied and checked, no fewer than 23 confirmed victories were awarded to the pilots of the 23rd. Only two P-40s were lost, both as a result of running out of fuel on their way home, and both downed pilots returned safely to base. It was the highest scoring mission in 23rd FG history. Capt John Hampshire of the 75th led all pilots with three confirmed kills, bringing his total to five. Also reaching ace status were 1Lt Charles DuBois of the 76th with two victories and 1Lt John 'Moe' Lombard of the 16th with one. Future aces who scored on the mission were Maj Holloway of the 76th FS and Capt Goss of the 16th FS with two each, plus Lt Col Clinton D 'Casey' Vincent (CATF operations officer), 1Lt Dallas Clinger of the 16th FS and 1Lt Marvin Lubner of the 76th FS with one apiece. Col Scott also recorded two victories.

ACES' FAREWELL

Big changes occurred on 5 December. That morning, former AVG pilots 'Tex' Hill, Ed Rector, 'Gil' Bright and Charlie Sawyer boarded a transport in Kunming to begin their long-awaited journey home to the US. At that time, Hill was the leading active ace in the CBI with 11.75 victories, and Rector was not far behind with 6.75 kills. Both men would return to China later in the war to serve a stint as CO of the 23rd FG. The last remaining AVG pilot, 74th FS commander Maj Frank Schiel, was killed later that same day flying a mission in a Lockheed F-4 Lightning photo-reconnaissance aircraft that fell victim to bad weather.

Three new squadron commanders took over from them, namely Capt 'Ajax' Baumler in the 74th FS, Maj John Alison in the 75th FS and Maj Bruce Holloway in the 76th FS. When Col Scott returned to the US a month later, Holloway replaced him as CO of the 23rd FG, and a

DAISY MAE was one of two Lockheed F-4s of the 9th Photo-Reconnaissance Squadron attached to the 23rd FG in 1942. Maj Frank Schiel, commander of the 74th FS, was killed flying one during a weather reconnaissance mission on 5 December 1942 (*Doug Erickson*)

Groundcrewman George Spencer stands next to P-40K '110' of the 76th FS. Its regular pilot was Capt Jeffery Wellborn, who scored the group's only solo P-43 victory. The extended vertical fin of the P-40K, intended to counteract the torque of its uprated Allison engine, is clearly visible in this shot (*George Spencer*)

Maj Harry M Pike of the 16th FS shot down this Ki-48 bomber of the 90th Sentai over Kweilin in the early morning darkness on 23 November 1942. Lacking radar-guided ground control, pilots of the 23rd FG enjoyed only limited success during night interceptions (*G W Hazlett*)

newcomer to China in the form of Capt Grant Mahony assumed command of the 76th FS.

The last major engagement of 1942 for the 23rd FG came at Yunnanyi. The 16th FS, now led by Maj George Hazlett, had deployed to the advanced 'Hump' base near the Burma border on Christmas Eve because Gen Chennault had a hunch that the airfield was about to be attacked by the Japanese. As usual, he was right, for the enemy caught the 16th FS on the ground on Christmas afternoon – fortunately none of its aeroplanes was hit. Several hours later Col Scott arrived from Kunming with instructions to prevent any further surprise attacks from taking place.

Scott sent up a two-aeroplane patrol at first light on 26 December, and increased the size of his standing patrol throughout the morning. By 1400 hrs the full squadron was airborne, and just before 1500 hrs nine twin-engined Ki-21 'Sally' bombers with ten Ki-43 escorts were spotted crossing the Mekong River from Burma at 17,000 ft. A flight of four, led by 16th FS operations officer Maj Harry Pike, was the first to make contact, and it successfully drew the escort fighters away from the bombers. Then Col Scott and Maj Hazlett led two more flights in to attack the now defenceless Ki-21s.

One of the pilots who took part in the mission was Capt Bob Liles. He recalled that a good friend of his in the 16th FS, Lt Bob Mooney, had been delayed on the deployment to Yunnanyi, and did not arrive until the day of the fight. Liles told this story;

'Just as I was taxiing out to take off, I saw Bob Mooney land. I saw him pull his clothes bag out of the aeroplane. He was trying to get refuelled so that he could get in on the mission. I left. We were patrolling some miles south of the field, anticipating the Jap attack. Maj Pike was leading my flight, and Hazlett the other. Just as we were about ready to sail into them, a lone aeroplane came streaking up from base, and it was Mooney. I recognised his P-40. He went past me going pretty fast. At that point we went right into these Zeros and bombers.

'I was getting ready to shoot at a Zero, moving to the right. Mooney picked on one going to the left. We never did actually form up as an element and start fighting that way. That was the last time I saw him. He was shot down that day. Most of the Jap aeroplanes that came in that day were shot down, too. When I landed, someone told me Mooney was down, so I quickly got a Jeep and driver and we went out west of Yunnanyi to look for him. We knew only approximately where he was. The Chinese told us about the location, so when we got there I saw him being carried on a door.'

Lt Mooney was still alive when Liles found him, but the young pilot died that night. Lt Lewellyn Couch was also shot down that same day, but

The 16th FS produced quite a number of outstanding leaders, but none were more respected than Maj Harry B Pike. After a stint as CO of the 16th FS, Pike moved up to 23rd FG headquarters, but was shot down and taken prisoner in September 1943 (*George Barnes*)

The 16th FS armament crew bore-sites an unusual-looking P-40E. Note the hard break between the top and bottom camouflage colours and the lack of a fuselage star. Its number ('52' or '62') is also non-standard for the 16th FS (*Jack Muller*)

The 23rd FG began to receive new P-40Ks in October 1942. Judging from the expressions of Sgt Leon Klesman, left, and his unidentified buddy, this 74th FS bird ('47') acquired a nickname that applied as much to its crewmen as to the aircraft itself. Note the crude application of the sharksmouth marking (*Leon Klesman*)

he survived with a twisted knee. On the plus side, the 16th FS was credited with ten victories, and Col Scott had managed to add one more to his total. Bob Liles, who would go on to score five victories and serve as commander of the 16th for more than a year, recorded his first confirmed kill, plus a probable, and Dallas Clinger got his fourth during the course of the mission.

By the time 1942 ended, the 23rd FG had tallied 97 confirmed victories in six months of combat. The 16th FS led the way with 35 victories, the 75th and 76th were tied with 29 each and the 74th had four.

The first three months of 1943 were relatively quiet in China, as the CATF stockpiled supplies at its advance bases and wedged in missions during sporadic periods of acceptable flying weather. Meanwhile, new P-40K fighters began arriving in greater numbers, and the 23rd FG was able to begin retiring its old AVG 'sharks' to training units in India.

ACTION IN THE EAST

The 23rd FG enjoyed a relatively quiet period during the first three months of 1943, with claims for aerial combat submitted on just two dates in January, and none in February or March. At this time, however, political forces were at work in Washington, D.C., to put greater emphasis on the air war in China. The first move was to raise the status of Chennault's organisation, and accordingly on 10 March 1943 the Fourteenth Air Force was activated in Kunming to replace the CATF, with Chennault as its commanding officer.

On that day, he reported his command having 103 P-40s, of which 65 were assigned to his five fighter squadrons and the rest were in various states of assembly and repair at the factory facilities in Kunming. More units would arrive in the coming months, but for the time being the war went on as before for Chennault's pilots.

The quiet period drew to a close in late March 1943, when Chennault deployed his squadrons on both fronts in preparation for resuming offensive operations against the Japanese. He moved the 74th FS, now under the command of Capt John Lombard, to Yunnanyi, where it could

Gen H H 'Hap' Arnold (left), chief of the USAAF, inspects 23rd FG P-40s with Brig Gen Chennault at Kunming in February 1943. A month later, Arnold would approve orders creating the Fourteenth Air Force to replace the CATF in China, with Chennault as its commanding officer (*Bruce Holloway*)

protect the 'Hump' corridor and also strike at the Japanese in northern Burma. The 16th FS, under new commander Maj Hal Pike, and one flight of the 76th FS went to Kweilin, and the 75th moved to nearby Lingling. From these bases, they could hit the Japanese in the Hankow and Canton/Hong Kong areas. Meanwhile, the bulk of the 76th would remain at Kunming for air defence and offensive missions into Indochina.

The 75th FS dominated aerial combat in April, with one of the legendary figures of the China air war emerging during this period. Capt John Hampshire scored his sixth victory on the first day of the month over Lingling, followed by claims for two more kills on 24 April which saw him take the scoring lead among active pilots in the CBI. He described the action in a letter he sent to his father back home in Grants Pass, Oregon, on the 25th. Hampshire wrote;

'Yesterday, the Japanese paid us another visit, and it was a dilly. They really sent in the first team this time, and they had the most beautiful air discipline I have ever seen. There were 30 or so of them, all fighters, and it was impossible to catch anyone asleep or by itself, so it was mighty tough going for awhile. When the smoke cleared, we had shot down five, and we didn't lose any, so it wasn't a bad day, although it certainly could have been better. The fight was a fairly long one, and just when it was ending, one of their twin-engined fighters flew over and dropped out a bunch of pamphlets – they challenged us to a "decisive air battle".

'The monkey that dropped the pamphlets ran into a little hard luck on the way home. For a while it looked like I'd never catch him, but I finally did after chasing him for a hundred miles. So that ended the show for that day – I got two.'

The JAAF turned the tables on the 23rd FG on 26 April. At Yunnanyi, a breakdown in the warning net near the Salween River allowed a force of enemy bombers and fighters to catch Lombard's 74th FS on the ground

Hundreds of names of CATF personnel were embroidered into this flag, which the staff presented to Brig Gen Chennault in early 1943. The men in the photograph are, from left to right, Col C D 'Casey' Vincent, Maj 'Ajax' Baumler, Lt Col Bruce Holloway, Maj Aubrey Strickland and Brig Gen Chennault (*Bruce Holloway*)

and put the unit temporarily out of action. The 16th and 75th FSs pulled back to Yunnanyi and Kunming, respectively, from their eastern bases, as further trouble was expected.

It duly arrived on 28 April, but this time the Japanese target was Kunming, which had not been bombed in daylight since the first AVG mission of 20 December 1941. The bombers managed to reach the airfield and bomb it, but they paid a high price at the hands of the 75th on their way home. Again, the warning net had failed to give the group sufficient time to attack the aircraft inbound, so Lt Col John Alison led his squadron on an interception course that allowed the P-40s to catch the formation on its return flight to Burma. One of the 75th FS pilots involved was Capt Hollis Blackstone, who recalled;

'My buddy, Capt John Hampshire, and I joined up. Shortly afterwards, our CO, Lt Col Johnny Alison, spotted the Japs and gave us a heading. From that bearing I knew they were heading for Lashio, Burma. "Hamp" and I spotted two of our fighters milling around, and we waggled our wings for them to join up. I picked out Lt Joe Griffin, and I believe "Hamp" got Lt Mack Mitchell. After awhile we could see a black line across the horizon. This turned out to be 21 Jap bombers in perfect vee formation. A little later we saw, like a swarm of bees, three umbrellas of Jap fighters with one honcho way above – 35 fighters in all.

'Johnny Alison made the first attack and downed one of them, if I recall it right. By then the four of us had caught up with the Japs, at which point all hell broke loose. Starting out with an altitude advantage, we tore into the melee with our 0.50-cals ablaze. Pieces flew off one of the Zeros and smoke poured out of another. But right then we saw eight diving on us and had to take evasive action. We did that with a steep banking dive, pulling away from the bombers' line of flight. It was at this point that we realised the Zeros would only follow us so far before going back to their protective escort of the bombers. Unmolested, we regained altitude and hit again.

'I can't recall how many firing passes I made, but I shot down at least one more Jap aeroplane. During this time we were joined by Maj Ed Goss, with Lt Roger Pryor on his wing. Joe and I spotted six or eight Zeros and dived on them, our 0.50s blazing. Immediately some of them started a steep climb, while others dived. The one I was chasing burst into flames. While watching him go down and looking for Joe, whom I had lost contact with, I saw some more Japs coming after me but I finally managed to elude them.

'I got some altitude again. Ahead and below me, I spotted a buddy I assumed to be Joe (it was) hot after a Jap with his guns blazing. What he didn't see was two Japs coming after him. I in turn dove after them and blasted one. I then saw two rips appear across the top of my left wing, shattering my aileron. My control stick was vibrating badly, I was low on gas and about out of ammo. Nevertheless, I made it home. The beautiful and most amazing part of this mission was the fact that we didn't lose a single aeroplane, in spite of the great odds against us.'

The 23rd FG's tally for the mission was 11 confirmed and eight probables. Blackstone was credited with two destroyed and one probable. A notable scorer was Maj Ed Goss, who had transferred to the 75th from the 16th in preparation for assuming command of the squadron from Alison. Goss' single victory brought his total to five, and added him to the

Bombed up for a ground attack mission, P-40K '23' of the 16th FS was assigned to Lt Robert A O'Neill. Amongst the markings applied to the fighter was the nickname *DEANIE III* on the cowling, the pilot's name and three victory flags beneath the windscreen, and starred hubcaps – the latter were common on 16th FS P-40s during this period (*Jack Muller*)

ace roster. Future aces scoring in the fight included Pryor and Griffin, who got one kill each. Meanwhile, Charles DuBois of the 76th scored his sixth, and last, victory in the fight, and Hampshire stretched his record to 11 confirmed by scoring twice.

John Hampshire's luck ran out four days later. By then, the 75th had moved back to Lingling and was preparing to resume offensive operations. On 2 May the Japanese beat them to the punch by sending a large force of fighters from the 25th and 33rd Sentais down from Hankow to attack Lingling. Lt Col Alison scrambled 16 P-40s to challenge them, and the two formations met not far from the airfield. Records conflict on the exact sequence of events, but it appears that 1Lt Don Brookfield scored a victory in the initial engagement, and then the P-40s began chasing the enemy back toward Hankow. Japanese fighters continued to fall on the flight north, with Hampshire getting two near Changsha. Alison wrote a description of what happened next in a letter to Hampshire's father;

'When it was over, Johnny rejoined my formation, and as he pulled in close on my wing I could see a big grin on his face. He told me on the radio that he had followed his man down and saw him crash and burn. We then headed north, and after a very long chase intercepted a formation of Jap fighters which had been strafing a Chinese town. It must have been a lucky shot from a Zero that got him, as none of us saw it happen. John set his aeroplane down in a river and the Chinese took him to the nearest hospital. He died before he could reach adequate medical attention.'

Hampshire had crashed near a Chinese army outpost, which quickly relayed word back to Lingling that the pilot was wounded but alive. 75th FS flight surgeon Capt Ray Spritzler told Alison he wanted to fly to the crash site and see if he could help Hampshire. When Lt Joe Griffin volunteered to fly Spritzler there in the baggage compartment of a P-43, Alison reluctantly agreed. Spritzler planned to bale out over the crash site.

Shortly after the P-43 took off, the Chinese relayed another message – Hampshire had died. Alison tried unsuccessfully to recall Griffin by radio, but bad weather forced the P-43 to land at an unmanned airstrip near a

The P-43A Lancer saw limited service with the 23rd FG during 1942-43. This particular aircraft was assigned to group headquarters, which had the fighter converted into a photo-reconnaissance platform – note the opening for the camera lens in the bottom of the fuselage immediately behind the groundcrewman holding the bulky camera. The lack of self-sealing fuel tanks made the Lancer too dangerous to fly in aerial combat with the JAAF (*Bruce Holloway*)

Chinese village. Griffin and Spritzler returned to Lingling the next morning. Joe Griffin scored three victories in China and got four more in the ETO during 1944 while serving as a squadron CO in the 367th FG.

Hampshire's two kills on 2 May gave him a total of 13 confirmed victories, tying him with Bob Neale of the AVG as the top-scoring US P-40 pilot of the war. Only 23rd FG commander Col Bruce Holloway would join them at the top of the pile.

MORE PUNCH FOR THE FOURTEENTH AIR FORCE

The first step in the build up of the Fourteenth Air Force was the addition of a heavy-bomber unit in the form of the 308th BG. Equipped with four-

B-24 Liberator heavy bombers of the 308th BG pass overhead a Fourteenth Air Force fighter base in mid-1943. This unit arrived in China in the spring of 1943 as part of the Fourteenth Air Force build-up in-theatre, and the 23rd FG escorted its B-24s on numerous occasions through to VJ-Day (*Molesworth collection*)

This poor quality photograph shows significant P-40K *Poco Lobo* of Capt James W Little, who was a seven-victory ace with the 75th FS (*Rick Garfield*)

Pilots of the 74th FS pose with a new P-40K at Kunming in early 1943. In the front row, from left to right, are R Turner, R Morrison, C Bair, W Crooks, R Lucia (PoW), W Smith (behind Lucia), A Cruikshank, J Hinton, T Shapou and T Jeffreys. Sat on the nose of the fighter are F Ladd, D Mitchell and C Crysler, whilst on its wing, from left to right, are L Jones, W Hawkins, D Anderson, C Bunch and W Wanner (*Leon Klesman*)

engine B-24D Liberators, the 308th flew its first mission out of Kunming on 4 May 1943 when it targeted Samah Bay on Hainan Island, in the South China Sea. The B-24s encountered light flak and no JAAF fighters over the target. Then, on 8 May, the Liberators joined B-25s of the 11th BS and 24 P-40s of the 16th and 75th FSs in a strike against Canton. The complex mission plan called for the long-range B-24s to fly to the target directly from Kunming, while the rest of the strike force would stage through Kweilin and meet B-24s just prior to reaching the target area.

The mission went according to plan, catching the Japanese at Canton by surprise. Enemy fighters were spotted taking off from White Cloud airfield during the attack, so the P-40s stayed in the area to hold them off while the bombers withdrew. A wild 20-minute air battle ensued, and when it was over the 23rd FG pilots tallied 13 'Oscars' and 'Nates' destroyed, plus five probables. Among the victories was an 'Oscar' downed

by 1Lt Jim Little of the 75th FS, giving him his fifth kill. The new ace would score twice more a week later, and then wait seven years before getting another chance.

On 27 June 1950, Little claimed one of the first victories of the Korean War when he destroyed a North Korean La-7 fighter while flying an F-82G Twin Mustang nightfighter.

In addition, Lt Col John Alison was credited with his fifth kill on 8 May. Alison would soon leave China for an important new assignment to help form the 1st Air Commando Group, but like Little, he first would add to his score.

The 23rd FG shuffled its fighter squadrons on 11 May, moving the 74th and 76th FSs to the eastern bases at Lingling and Kweilin, while pulling back the 75th FS to Kunming and putting the 16th at Yunnanyi. By 15 May, the 75th was settled at Kunming, and the 74th FS was at Chanyi waiting for the base at Kweilin to be prepared for its arrival.

The warning net came alive that morning with reports of a large enemy force approaching Kunming from Burma, and at 0910 hrs Col Holloway led a patrol out to look for the raiders. The three P-40s were 60 miles from base, and at 23,000 ft, when Holloway looked up to see a massive (for China) force of 30 Ki-48 'Lily' bombers approaching at 26,000 ft, escorted by 23 Ki-43 'Oscars' of the 64th Sentai above them – the latter were stepped up to 30,000 ft. Holloway climbed as he called in the raid to Kunming, and ordered Maj Ed Goss to scramble his 75th FS to intercept.

Holloway, with Maj Roland Wilcox and Lt Charles Crysler on his wing, clawed his way to 28,000 ft and turned in behind the formation to attack the escorts. By that time, the 'Lilys' were making their run over Kunming air base, but fortunately their bombs went wide and did little damage. Holloway wrote in his dairy;

'About the time the bombs dropped, we went in for our first attack. Two flights of the 75th were in position and did likewise. Wilcox got a Zero immediately, and so did Crysler. They both went straight down into the lake. I picked out a Zero but don't know if I got him or not – think I did. Our surprise was gone, so we pulled out and climbed back up to 27,000 ft.

'Our enemies made a slow turn to the left, and we went in again. By this time we had about 15 P-40s in the fight, and it was getting mixed up pretty

These three pilots from 23rd FG Headquarters were the first to intercept when Japanese bombers attacked Kunming on 15 May 1943, and they duly scored eight victories between them. They are, from left to right, Maj Roland Wilcox, who was credited with three fighters destroyed, Col Bruce Holloway, who got a fighter and a bomber, and Lt Charles Crysler, who also got three fighters. Brig Gen Chennault's pet dachshund 'Joe' shares the cockpit with Holloway (*Doug Wilcox*)

Capt Dallas Clinger flew P-40K '48' after he transferred from the 16th to the 74th FS in early 1943. The rudder art, similar to that seen on his previous P-40E-1, reflects both Clinger's Wyoming cowboy roots and also his opinion of his enemy. He had the fabric skin on the rudder removed so that he could take it home with him when he completed his combat tour (*Bill Hawkins*)

good. The bombers were keeping perfect formation, but pretty soon there were a couple of stragglers (probably crippled). It didn't take long to get these. Somebody polished off one of them, and I moved in behind the other and blew him all to hell. He caught fire, spun to the right about three times, and exploded. This was at about 25,000 ft.

'We kept working on the Zeros, which were pretty well broken up and headed for home in a scattered, demoralised fashion. I saw somebody chasing one, so I joined him. We chased him lower and lower, coordinating our attacks until he was finally flying right on the ground. He successfully dodged us about six times, but finally we got him cornered in the end of the valley. Lt Little closed in on him from the left, and I came in almost directly behind. He pulled sharply right, and I got him with a full deflection shot. He pulled up, flipped over and went straight into the ground – and made a pretty fire.

'I didn't see any more Japs, but the net was telling us about a second wave coming in. I climbed back to 25,000 ft over the field and ordered Lombard (74th FS commander), who was standing by at Chanyi waiting to go eat, to send three of his flights down immediately. I stayed over the field with headquarters and a few of the 75th until the red (74th FS) flights arrived from Chanyi. I then ordered all the whites (75th FS) to Yankai for a drink.'

The score for the day was 16 confirmed destroyed and nine probables. One of the Ki-43 pilots from the 64th Sentai who went down was Lt Takeshi Endo, commander of the 3rd Chutai. No P-40s were lost.

As a result of the action, the 23rd FG added another ace to its growing list. Capt Dallas Clinger of the 74th FS was able to make contact with the fleeing Japanese formation at the end of the battle, claiming one 'Oscar' destroyed plus a probable. Not only were these the first claims made by a 74th FS pilot in 1943, but they also made Clinger an ace with five victories. After the 74th completed its move to Kweilin on 19 May, its pilots would get plenty of opportunities to add to their scores.

In early May 1943, Japanese ground forces at Hankow commenced a campaign with the hope of taking China out of the war. In a two-pronged attack, one force headed westward up the Yangtze River toward Chungking, while the other moved south from Tungting Lake (Donting Hu) along the Hsiang River (Xiang Jiang). The latter army's primary objective was to capture the pesky Fourteenth Air Force's eastern airfields at Hengyang, Lingling and Kweilin. Neither thrust was destined to succeed, thanks in part to the work of the 74th and 76th FSs in support of Chinese forces at Changsha.

The two units, organised as the East China Task Force under the control of Col Casey Vincent, immediately commenced offensive operations against the advancing Japanese armies. On 23 May, Maj Lombard led two flights of his 74th FS from Kweilin to Hengyang to operate from that advanced base.

On that same day Maj Grant Mahony became an ace – a longtime goal of his. Leading nine P-40s on a strafing mission to Ichang (a Yangtze River town northwest of Tungting Lake), Mahony encountered a single Ki-27 'Nate' fighter and shot it down. He also destroyed two 'Nates' parked on the airfield at Ichang, and his flight shot up four trucks and a fuel dump.

The aggressive Maj Mahony would leave for home on 9 June after 19 months in combat. He returned to the CBI to fly with John Alison in the 1st Air Commando Group and then began a third tour in the Pacific Theatre late in the war. There, on 3 January 1945, he was killed during a strafing mission in a P-38.

The fighting continued in east China throughout June 1943, and as the 23rd FG approached its first birthday, the unit suffered the loss of one of its top aces. On the morning of 20 June, Maj John Lombard set out from Hengyang to check weather conditions north of Tungting Lake. The seven-victory ace was caught under a dropping overcast and crashed into a mountainside. He died one day short of his 24th birthday.

The weather was bad all over China on 4 July 1943 – the first anniversary of the 23rd FG. At Kweilin, the 74th FS hostel nearly flooded in a torrent of rain. The men of the 75th FS enjoyed an extra egg for breakfast and a glass of 'Sham-Shu' (the local Chinese firewater) with their dinners. Throughout

Col Bruce Holloway, second from right, makes a toast at a banquet in Kunming in July 1943 to mark the first birthday of the 23rd FG. Of Brig Gen Chennault, sat fourth from left, Holloway noted on the back of this photograph, 'typical expression on "The Old Man's" face'. The Chinese officer is Gen C P Mow (*Bruce Holloway*)

the group, men had time to reflect on their successes over the past year. They had held the line against the Japanese in east China while protecting their end of the 'Hump' from enemy attack, and the pilots had scored 171 confirmed victories in the process. On the other hand, nothing much had changed for the better either. The older P-40s had given way to newer K- and M-models, but the aeroplanes were still few in number and badly worn. Fuel and ammunition were still in short supply, not to mention luxuries such as fresh meat, soap and uniforms. Even worse, mail deliveries remained sporadic at best.

In Kunming, Col Bruce Holloway tried to make light of the situation in his typical droll manner during a first anniversary party for 23rd FG personnel. A year earlier when the unit was activated, he noted, there was not a single American magazine at Kunming for the guys to read. Now they had several. Nobody laughed.

ENTER THE P-38

On a quiet day in July 1943, five twin-engined fighters landed at Kunming airfield, having just flown across the 'Hump' from India. Their sleek, twin-boom design made them immediately recognisable as Lockheed Lightnings, but these were different from the F-4 photo-reconnaissance versions that had been flying in China since the previous autumn. These were brand-new P-38Gs, considered at that time to be the best operational fighter aircraft in the USAAF inventory.

The five P-38s and their pilots were the advance element of a full squadron of Lightnings – the 449th FS – that was on its way to China. Boasting long-range and high-altitude performance equal to the F-4, these aeroplanes far exceeded the capabilities of the P-40. In addition,

"LITTLE TOOTSIE" **was one of the original P-38Gs that the 449th FS flew from North Africa to China, arriving in the summer of 1943. The squadron served for three months under the command of the 23rd FG, scoring its first victory on 24 July over Kweilin (***A Roscetti***)**

Six-victory ace Maj Ed Goss got his start in China with the 16th FS, before transferring to the 75th FS as its commanding officer in May 1943. When the 449th FS arrived in China, he was attached to lead the squadron temporarily while teaching its pilots how to fight 'Chennault-style' in their P-38s (*Mrs E R Goss*)

P-40s of the 75th and 76th FSs stand alert at Kunming in mid-1943. '152' displays the flying shark badge of the 75th FS on its rudder and national insignia overpainted on the fuselage and uppersurface of its right wing. Note the all important C-87 Liberator tanker in the background (*Everett Hyatt*)

P-38Gs carried heavy armament, with a 20 mm cannon and four 0.50-cal machine guns grouped in the nose. The P-38's only drawback, as Gen Chennault saw it, was that its turbocharged Allison engines used too much of the Fourteenth Air Force's precious gasoline.

By the third week in July, all of the 449th FS's Lightnings had arrived in Kunming. The squadron commander, Capt Sam L Palmer, and several other pilots had combat experience flying the P-38 in the Mediterranean theatre. In fact Palmer had scored a probable victory in the MTO that spring. The rest were fresh out of training, however, having been drawn from a pool of replacement pilots in North Africa. Maj Ed Goss of the 75th FS was attached to the 449th to teach the pilots Chennault-style air tactics and lead them in their initial combat missions. Some China hands recall the P-38 pilots as being none too receptive to Goss's advice.

On 23 July, the 449th FS flew its P-38s to Kweilin to join the Fourteenth Air Force's Forward Echelon under the command of Col Casey Vincent. The squadron's arrival was fortuitous because the Japanese attacked Lingling and Hengyang that same day as they kicked off a new air offensive aimed at destroying Fourteenth Air Force bases and units in east China. But as in the past, the expectations of the Japanese commanders would far exceed their units' ability to do the job. Over the next week, Vincent's fighter pilots would claim no fewer than 54 confirmed victories, while losing just six fighters and three pilots in return.

On the morning of 23 July, the JAAF sent a mixed formation of bombers and fighters from Hankow to attack Hengyang and Lingling. The enemy aircraft took a roundabout route to their targets, and flights from the 76th FS scrambled from both bases to meet them. The Lingling-based P-40s made first contact about 50 kilometres southeast of the field. Under their aggressive attack, the Japanese bombers jettisoned their ordnance and ran for home, while their 'Oscar' escorts tangled with the P-40s. Meanwhile, a large flight of 18 P-40s from the 74th FS arrived from Kweilin and joined the fight.

The 23rd FG pilots were credited with two bombers and five fighters destroyed in this engagement, with three kills going to 76th FS flight leader Capt Lee Manbeck and another to future ace 2Lt Stephen Bonner.

By the time the Japanese raiders reached Hengyang, two more flights of P-40s from the 76th FS were waiting for them at 28,000 ft, led by 1Lts J M 'Willie' Williams and John S Stewart. When the latter pilot's oxygen system began to fail, he descended to 20,000 ft and duly spotted the incoming enemy bombers. Calling Williams down to take on the 'Oscar' escorts, Stewart ploughed into the bomber formation head-on.

His first victim staggered and fell, while gunners from the other bombers fired wildly at the attacking P-40. Stewart shot down a second bomber and was firing on a third when his own aeroplane was hit hard. He broke off the attack and headed back to Hengyang, where he had to make a belly landing because his landing gear refused to come down. Later, mechanics counted 167 bullet holes in Stewart's P-40K, which he had named *Lynn II* for his wife. Williams and 2Lt Dick Templeton were able to confirm two 'Oscars' destroyed in the fight as well.

That afternoon, another wave of enemy aircraft was reported on its way toward Hengyang and Lingling, and again the P-40 defenders rose to do battle, led this time by Capt Marvin Lubner. At the same time, Col Casey Vincent led six P-40s up from Kweilin, while Col Bruce Holloway flew in to Lingling, gassed up, and took off again to join the fight. The P-40 pilots encountered a large formation, and claimed six destroyed for no losses. Among the victories was a bomber credited to Vincent (his fifth), which added his name to the list of aces.

The next morning, 24 July, the Japanese struck Chennault's eastern bases again, this time from both Hankow to the north and from Canton down south. The 76th added eight victories to its tally at Lingling, again for no losses, and a flight from the 74th that had scrambled from Kweilin scored two more victories but lost one pilot killed in the process.

Meanwhile, a flight of eight Oscars from Canton managed to approach within 38 miles of Kweilin before they were spotted. P-40s and P-38s were hastily scrambled, but they were caught from above by the Ki-43 escorts. One P-38 was shot down, but the 23rd FG pilots quickly managed to gain the upper hand and destroy six of the eight attackers. Col Holloway shot down one of the 'Oscars' for his tenth victory. 1Lt Lewden M Enslen of the 449th FS was also on the scoresheet, claiming the first kill credited to a P-38 pilot in China (*text continues on page 65*).

Several of the P-40Ks assigned to the 74th FS carried risqué rudder art, such as *MISSY WONG from HONG KONG*, during 1943-44. Unfortunately, the identity of the artist who created these works remains unknown. Note how the camouflage on the vertical tail has been repainted to cover the aircraft's serial number (*Leon Klesman*)

COLOUR PLATES

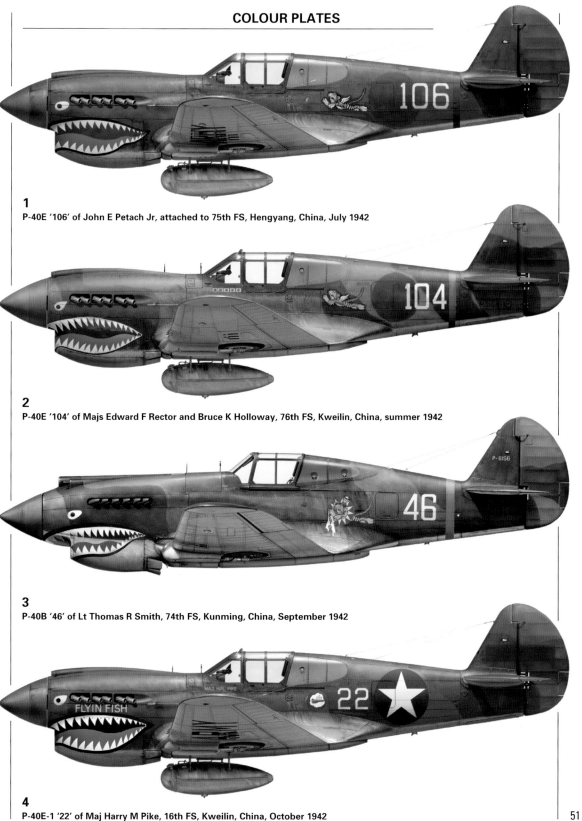

1
P-40E '106' of John E Petach Jr, attached to 75th FS, Hengyang, China, July 1942

2
P-40E '104' of Majs Edward F Rector and Bruce K Holloway, 76th FS, Kweilin, China, summer 1942

3
P-40B '46' of Lt Thomas R Smith, 74th FS, Kunming, China, September 1942

4
P-40E-1 '22' of Maj Harry M Pike, 16th FS, Kweilin, China, October 1942

5
P-43A '149' of the 76th FS, Kunming, China, late 1942

6
P-40K '7' of Col Robert L Scott, 23rd FG, Kunming, China, December 1942

7
P-40K '23' of Lt Robert A O'Neill, 16th FS/23rd FG, Chanyi, China, February 1943

8
P-40K '110' of Capt Jeffrey O Wellborn, 76th FS, Kunming, China, spring 1943

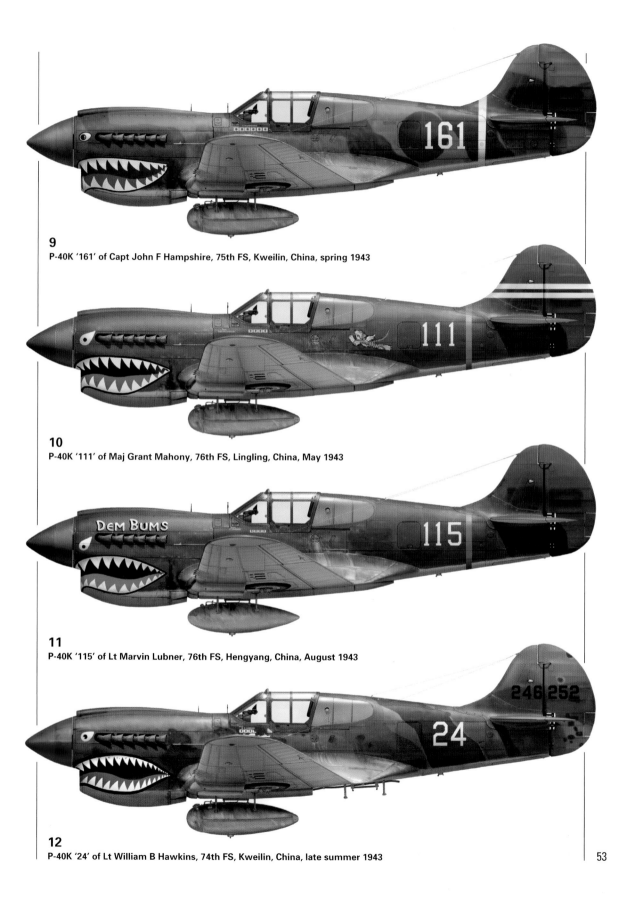

9
P-40K '161' of Capt John F Hampshire, 75th FS, Kweilin, China, spring 1943

10
P-40K '111' of Maj Grant Mahony, 76th FS, Lingling, China, May 1943

11
P-40K '115' of Lt Marvin Lubner, 76th FS, Hengyang, China, August 1943

12
P-40K '24' of Lt William B Hawkins, 74th FS, Kweilin, China, late summer 1943

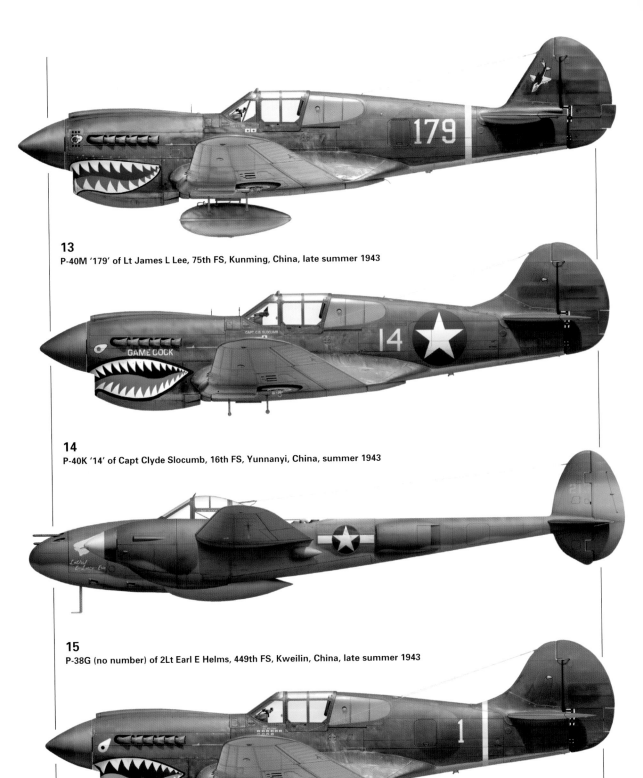

13
P-40M '179' of Lt James L Lee, 75th FS, Kunming, China, late summer 1943

14
P-40K '14' of Capt Clyde Slocumb, 16th FS, Yunnanyi, China, summer 1943

15
P-38G (no number) of 2Lt Earl E Helms, 449th FS, Kweilin, China, late summer 1943

16
P-40K '1' of Col Bruce Holloway, 23rd FG, Kweilin, China, September 1943

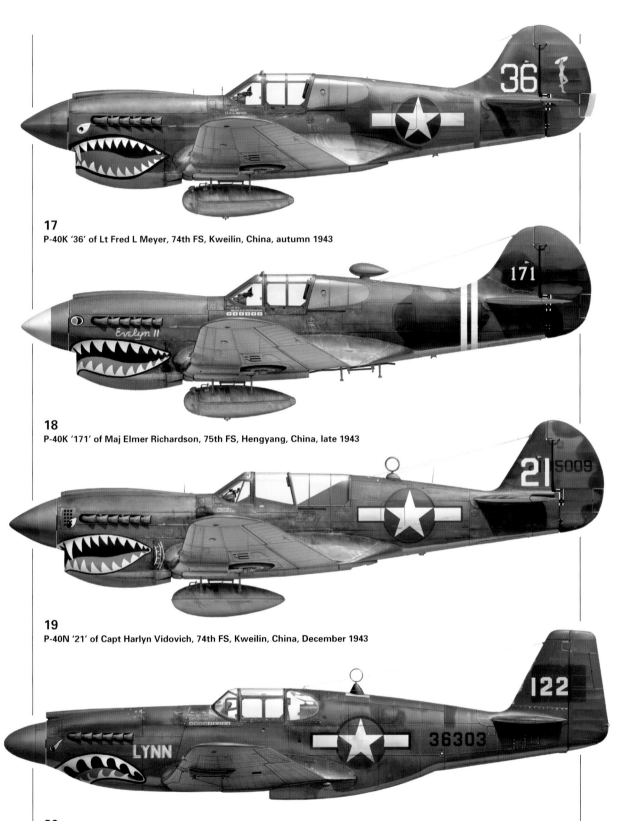

17
P-40K '36' of Lt Fred L Meyer, 74th FS, Kweilin, China, autumn 1943

18
P-40K '171' of Maj Elmer Richardson, 75th FS, Hengyang, China, late 1943

19
P-40N '21' of Capt Harlyn Vidovich, 74th FS, Kweilin, China, December 1943

20
P-51A '122' of Capt John S Stewart, 76th FS, Suichwan, China, February-March 1944

21
P-40N '45' of Maj Arthur Cruikshank, 74th FS, Hengyang, China, June 1944

22
P-40N '22' of Capt Charles E Cook Jr, 74th FS, Kweilin, China, summer 1944

23
P-51B '11' of Col David L Hill, 23rd FG, Kweilin, China, summer 1944

24
P-51C '103' of Lt Robert Schaeffer, 76th FS, Liuchow, China, autumn 1944

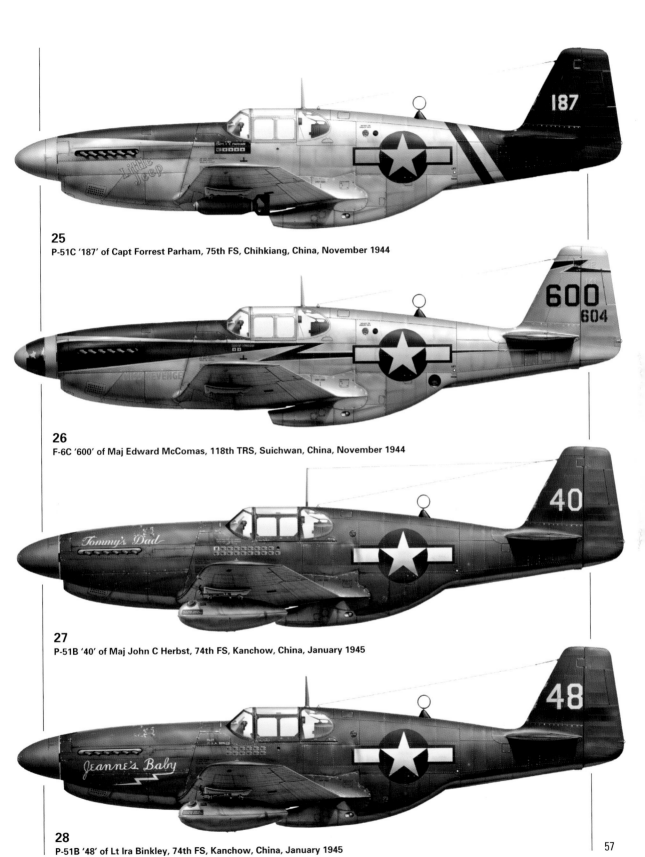

25
P-51C '187' of Capt Forrest Parham, 75th FS, Chihkiang, China, November 1944

26
F-6C '600' of Maj Edward McComas, 118th TRS, Suichwan, China, November 1944

27
P-51B '40' of Maj John C Herbst, 74th FS, Kanchow, China, January 1945

28
P-51B '48' of Lt Ira Binkley, 74th FS, Kanchow, China, January 1945

29
P-51D (no number) of Col Edward Rector, 23rd FG, Luliang, China, spring 1945

30
P-51D '125' of Lt Col Charles Older, 23rd FG HQ, Luliang, China, spring 1945

31
P-51C '113' of Lt Donald L Scott, 76th FS, Laohwangping, China, spring 1945

32
P-51C '591' of Lts Fred L Richardson Jr and Russell E Packard, 118th TRS, Chengkung, China, spring 1945

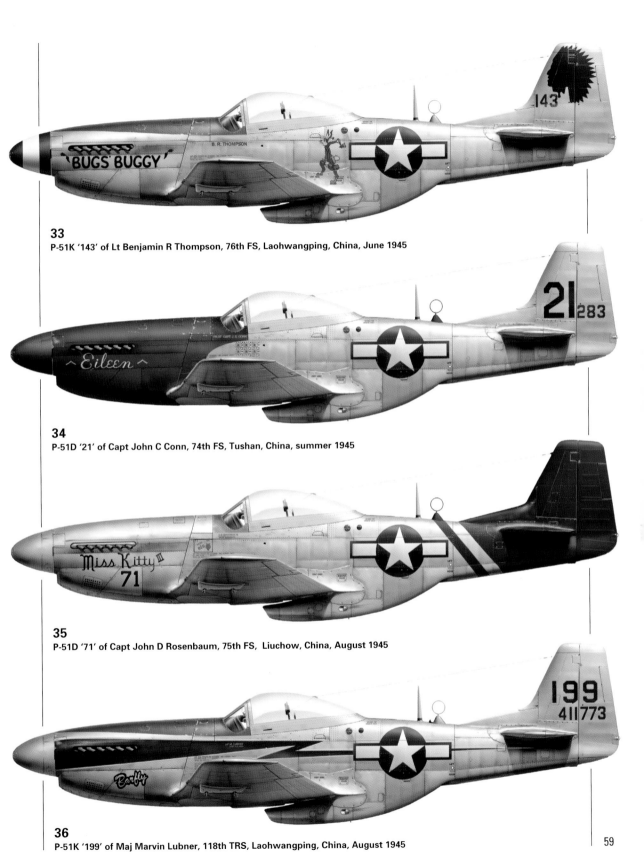

33
P-51K '143' of Lt Benjamin R Thompson, 76th FS, Laohwangping, China, June 1945

34
P-51D '21' of Capt John C Conn, 74th FS, Tushan, China, summer 1945

35
P-51D '71' of Capt John D Rosenbaum, 75th FS, Liuchow, China, August 1945

36
P-51K '199' of Maj Marvin Lubner, 118th TRS, Laohwangping, China, August 1945

1
23rd FG

2
16th FS

3
74th FS

4
75th FS

5
76th FS

6
118th TRS

1

2

3

4

MAP
From its air bases in China, the USAAF's Fourteenth Air Force could strike targets in the Japanese-held areas of Hankow, Canton/Hong Kong, French Indochina and Burma, as well as harassing Japanese shipping lanes in the South China Sea

Capt William B Hawkins flew P-40K-1 '24' (42-46252) during his tour with the 74th FS in 1942-43, gaining credit for three confirmed victories and one ship sunk whilst at the controls of the fighter. Note the aircraft's crude drop tank – almost certainly a Chinese-made item that was manufactured out of bamboo (*Bill Hawkins*)

More action followed on 25 July, when 15 Japanese fighters attempted to catch a flight of B-25s landing at Hengyang after their bombing mission to Hankow. Holloway had a patrol of P-40s waiting, just in case, and they knocked down two, plus three probables, for no losses. The B-25s, meanwhile, diverted to Kweilin and returned to Hengyang just before dusk to be ready for the next day's mission.

Five B-25s took off from Hengyang at 0500 hrs on 26 July to attack Hankow airfield once again. Their escorts were P-40s from the 74th and 75th FSs, which had sent seven aeroplanes from Kunming earlier in the week to bolster the eastern fighter force. After the B-25s had completed their bomb runs, a large force of Ki-43s attacked them, and several bombers sustained damage before the P-40s could intercede. A running fight ensued, in which Capt Elmer Richardson of the 75th FS claimed two destroyed and another future ace, 1Lt Lynn F Jones of the 74th FS, got one confirmed plus two probables.

Col Vincent sent his bombers and fighters to strike Hong Kong harbour on 27 and 28 July, with little opposition from the Japanese. The P-40s and P-38s went back to Hong Kong on the 29th, this time to rendezvous with 18 B-24s of the 308th BG flying from Kunming. Again, only a few Japanese defenders appeared, and the escorts easily held them off. Meanwhile, a JAAF force attacked Hengyang. An aggressive attack led by Capt Bill Grosvenor of the 75th FS threw off the bombers' aim, and no damage was done to the airfield.

The morning of 30 July signalled the end of the JAAF's offensive against Chennault's eastern airfields. The 3rd Air Division sent two formations from Hankow on different routes toward Hengyang, attempting to

76th FS pilots and groundcrew pose with two P-40Ks at Hengyang in the summer of 1943. Capt Bob Costello, squadron commander, is fourth from right in the front row. *CALVERT'S SPECIAL* (left) was a 75th FS aircraft that had possibly been reassigned to the 76th. At right is Capt Marv Lubner's *DEM BUMS* (*Glen Beneda*)

Maj Norval Bonawitz assumed command of the 74th FS in June 1943 after Maj 'Moe' Lombard was killed. Bonawitz shot down two Japanese bombers on 24 July 1943 at Lingling, and was promoted to 23rd FG commander later that year when Col Holloway returned to the US (*Bill Hawkins*)

confuse the defenders. Unfortunately for the Japanese aircrews, the Chinese warning net was able to plot both tracks accurately, so when they joined north of Hengyang for their final run into the target, the American pilots were in a perfect position to oppose them. Led by 1Lt Charlie Gordon of the 75th FS, the P-40s feinted toward a flight of 'Oscar' escorts, but then cut sharply into the bomber formation. Four bombers went down, including one each credited to Gordon, Capt Bill Grosvenor and 1Lt Ed Calvert of the 75th FS, plus 1Lt Vernon Kramer of the 76th FS. Lts Carter 'Porky' Sorenson of the 16th FS, Christopher 'Sully' Barrett of the 75th FS and Tom McMillan of the 76th FS each claimed an 'Oscar' destroyed. On the other side of the ledger, two P-40s were shot down and one pilot, Lt W S Epperson of the 75th FS, was killed.

It is impossible to determine whether heavy Japanese combat losses or the onset of bad weather was more responsible for the three-week lull in air fighting that followed. Col Vincent took the opportunity to rearrange his fighter forces, placing the full complement of 449th FS P-38s at Lingling and moving the 76th FS to Hengyang, along with two flights from the 16th FS.

The JAAF had a surprise in store for the P-40s' pilots as well. It was beginning to re-equip its fighter squadrons at Hankow with the new Nakajima Ki-44 'Tojo'. This aircraft would give the Japanese pilots a clear performance advantage over their P-40-equipped adversaries.

The 23rd FG's first encounter with the 'Tojos' came on 20 August 1943, when Col Holloway and Maj Norval Bonawitz, commander of the 74th FS, led 14 P-40s from Kweilin to intercept a raid coming in from Hankow. What they encountered was a fighter sweep by 20 Ki-44s flying at 30,000 ft or higher – well above the combat ceiling of the P-40s. The Warhawk pilots had no choice but to wait for the 'Tojos' to initiate battle on their own terms. This they did by diving down on straggling P-40s, taking a shot at them, and then zooming back up out of range – precisely the tactics preached by Chennault to his P-40 pilots. Two Curtiss fighters and their pilots were lost, but Capt Art Cruikshank of the 74th was able to claim two 'Tojos' destroyed.

The P-40s were in action again that afternoon, knocking down four 'Oscars' over Tien Ho airfield at Canton while escorting B-25s. Another Japanese attack on Hengyang the next day netted five more victories for the P-40s of the 76th FS against one loss. Col Bruce Holloway scored his 11th and 12th kills on these two missions, and his 13th, and last, victory came on 24 August during an escort mission. As he recorded in his diary, Holloway passed up the chance to become the all-time top-scoring American P-40 ace that day;

'We came in with the B-25s and attacked the airfield at Wuchang. The bombing was good. There were several Zeros still over the town, but all were working singly. I made a head-on run with one and shot him down – I could have gotten more but we stuck right with the B-25s and kept the Zeros off them so nobody got hit. We stayed with them for 75 to 100 miles south. At this time we ran across three B-24s up to the left, and they kept yelling about a Zero above them. I saw it and kept watching it – finally it dived down behind the B-24s, pulled up and started west. I turned around with my flight and climbed up fast behind him – a perfect sitter, so I held off and let my wingman (Lt Francis Beck of the 16th FS) move in and get him. We came on home and nothing else happened. All P-40s got back okay, and we accounted for ten Zeros confirmed and three probables.'

Two weeks later, Col Holloway would be promoted to temporary commander of the Forward Echelon while Vincent took leave in the US. This effectively ended Holloway's combat flying in China, Lt Col Norval Bonawitz duly replacing him as CO of the 23rd FG.

Of the ten victories reported on 24 August, two apiece were credited to Capt Art Cruikshank of the 74th FS and 1Lt John Stewart of the 76th FS, making both men aces.

Capt Arthur W Cruikshank Jr became the first ace of the 74th FS when he scored his fifth and sixth confirmed victories on 24 August 1943 while leading an escort for B-24s attacking Hankow. He would add two more victories during a short second tour in mid-1944, but was subsequently grounded after being shot down twice in quick succession by enemy ground fire on 15 and 26 June (*Jack Cook*)

The 76th FS added two more aces during a morning escort mission to Canton on 26 August, when Capt Marvin Lubner claimed one victory for a total of five and 1Lt Willie Williams got his fifth and sixth kills, plus a probable. The latter pilot described his last victory, which occurred as he was attempting to chase off an 'Oscar' that was attacking a battle-damaged Warhawk;

'I turned back, rolled over, and fired way ahead of the Zero. I knew I was out of range but hoped the Zero pilot would see my tracers. He did see them and pulled straight up. Climbing was the thing for a Jap to do, only this time I had altitude on him. When he got to the top of his climb I was almost in formation with him. All I had to do was pull the trigger and let those six 0.50-cals do the rest. He rolled over with black smoke pouring out of the aeroplane and went into the ground.'

The Forward Echelon continued to pound enemy targets in east China throughout mid-September, its P-40 pilots recording 16 victories up to the 15th of that month. Japanese attacks on the east China airbases had all but ceased by this time, although the JAAF did not officially call off its aerial offensive until 8 October. By that time, however, it had suffered yet another serious drubbing.

On 20 September, the warning net detected a Japanese formation approaching Kunming from Indochina, and P-40s of the 16th and 75th FSs scrambled to meet it. This sector of China had been quiet all summer, so the pilots were eager to see some action. Seven P-40s of the 16th FS at

Chengkung, led by Maj Bob Liles, made first contact with the raiders. 1Lt Bill Evans, who was flying in the 'tail-end Charlie' slot, recalled the action;

'We immediately dropped our external belly tanks and made a diving pass against the bombers on their "one o'clock position". On our first pass I almost collided with a flaming Zero shot down by Liles that was going in the opposite direction. I could almost see the expression on the Jap pilot's face as he went by. He was leaning forward as if he had been hit. We made three or four passes, and after our attack we were immediately jumped on by the Zeros. Then, shortly after, we got scattered fending off the attacking Zeros. I didn't see the bomber that I was credited with shooting down, but I do know that I got some hits.

'The bombers proceeded to Kunming without most of their escort, which at that time was keeping us busy, apparently assuming that our seven-aircraft formation was the only American opposition. When they arrived over Kunming, however, they were hit hard by the 75th FS.'

A confident-looking Maj Robert L Liles, commander of the 16th FS from July 1943 until well into 1944, scored five confirmed victories in China during one of the longest combat tours on record for a fighter pilot serving in the CBI (*George Barnes*)

The 23rd FG instituted new markings in the autumn of 1943, as shown here on this P-40M of the 75th FS. The fighter has a white spinner front, its aircraft number has been moved to the rudder and national insignias, with bars and a red border, have been applied. This Warhawk was assigned to Lt C S 'Sully' Barrett (*James L Lee*)

Indeed, the 75th FS did hit the bombers hard. Three flights, led by Capts Charlie Gordon, Bill Grosvenor and Roger Pryor, attacked out of the sun and scattered the bombers. Gordon was credited with one bomber destroyed and Pryor with two, both achieving ace status with their fifth victories. Their squadronmates shot down nine more, including two credited to future ace Grosvenor (who would get his fifth on 1 October over Haiphong). The few bombs that hit the airfield at Kunming caused minor damage and no casualties. 1Lt Lyndon R 'Deacon' Lewis was shot down, but he returned to base unhurt five days later.

While the 23rd FG was busy holding the line in eastern China, big changes were taking shape for the Fourteenth Air Force as the long-awaited build-up picked up steam with the decision to transfer the 51st FG from the Tenth Air Force to China. The move in early October 1943 added two full P-40 squadrons – the 25th and 26th – to Chennault's forces. At this point, the 16th FS was transferred back to the 51st FG, and the 449th was reassigned to the 51st as well, ending the P-38 unit's short stint with the 23rd FG.

Capt Paul Bell was the regular pilot of *GRAND SLAM*, a 74th FS P-40M that was assigned to the squadron in April 1943. The aeroplane apparently never carried a sharksmouth, as photographs taken both early and late in its combat life show it without the signature P-40 marking of the 23rd FG. Bell assumed command of the 74th FS in October 1943 (*Bill Hawkins*)

MUSTANGS JOIN THE BATTLE

In late October 'Tex' Hill showed up in Kunming, rested, healthy and ready to go back into action. Now wearing the silver eagles of a full colonel, Hill had spent the past year as commander of the Proving Ground Group at Eglin Field, in Florida. At Eglin, he had taken the opportunity to fly all the latest models of USAAF fighters, as well as the British Spitfire and various bombers as well.

The fighter that impressed Hill most at Eglin was the North American P-51 Mustang. As far back as December 1942, when the 23rd FG's ex-AVG P-40s were on their last legs, Col Casey Vincent had written a memo to Washington, D.C., listing the P-51 as his first choice when it came to supplying a replacement fighter for China. Hill's experience flying Mustangs in Florida confirmed the wisdom of Vincent's request. He had flown the P-51A, which was powered by the same Allison engine as in the P-40, and had been impressed by its speed, handling characteristics and long range. Shortly before leaving for China, Hill also had a chance to fly the new P-51B, and he found it had all the attributes of the A-model plus much better straightline speed and high-altitude performance.

Perhaps by coincidence, the first Mustangs began arriving in China at about the same time 'Tex' Hill returned. The pilots of the 76th FS were thrilled when they received word in early October that it would be the first

These well-worn P-51As were the first Mustangs to arrive in China, where they were assigned to the 76th FS following service with the 311th FBG in India. Their first mission was an uneventful bomber escort to Hankow from Suichuan flown on 23 November 1943 (*Bob Colbert*)

NORTH AMERICAN P-51 MUSTANG

In the spring of 1940, as the air war began to heat up over northern Europe, Great Britain sent a special purchasing commission to the United States to buy aircraft for the RAF. One of the commission's stops was at the California offices of a relatively new aircraft manufacturer, North American Aviation (NAA). The British representatives wanted NAA to build Curtiss P-40s for them under license, but J H 'Dutch' Kindelberger, president of the company, had another idea.

Knowing that a difference in production methods between Curtiss and NAA would make the P-40 difficult to build, and believing that his company could use the lessons learned in the opening months of the air war to design a fighter that would outperform the P-40, Kindelberger counter-offered to build an all-new fighter for the RAF. The commission reluctantly agreed, and the NAA design team went to work. They completed a preliminary design by late April, and the prototype aircraft, designated the NA-73, rolled out just four months later in the autumn of 1940.

The NA-73 design incorporated several key elements that would give the new aeroplane performance equal to or better than the British and German fighters of the period. The designers paid utmost attention to creating a very fast aircraft by giving it a laminar flow wing airfoil, streamlined fuselage lines created by the use of a new mathematical system known as the development of secondary curves, and a ventral radiator system that actually boosted forward thrust

via its ram-air effect. For a powerplant, they chose the most powerful American inline engine then available – the Allison V-1710 – even though it was essentially the same as the engine being used in the Bell P-39 and the Curtiss P-40.

In flight tests during the winter of 1940-41 the NA-73 produced the performance that Kindelberger had promised, and the RAF immediately ordered the aeroplane into full production as the Mustang I. On learning of the new fighter's high performance, the US Army bought two of the early production Mustangs, redesignated them XP-51s, and shipped them to Wright Field, Ohio, for testing. When the XP-51s passed all their flight tests, the Army issued an order to NAA for 460 P-51 fighters and 500 A-36 dive-bomber versions. With a top speed of 387 mph, it was faster than all other fighters of the period, including the British Spitfire and the German Bf 109E.

The Mustang I went into action over Europe in August 1942, supporting commando troops during their ill-fated raid on Dieppe, in France. By this time, the RAF had recognised the aircraft's one weakness – lack of high altitude performance. The Allison engine had been designed to produce maximum power at 15,000 ft, but the engines in British and German fighters allowed them to fight at much higher altitudes. To rectify the situation, Maj Tom Hitchcock, Army Air Force attaché in London, proposed mating the Mustang airframe with the powerful Rolls-Royce Merlin engine. The Merlin,

unit to re-equip with the new fighters to replace their ageing P-40s. Groundcrews were given maintenance manuals for the P-51A to study, and the pilots sought out any information they could find about their new mounts. The first aeroplanes arrived in Kunming on 17 October, and by the end of the week 15 of them were on hand.

Although new to China, the P-51As were not exactly new airframes. The 311th Fighter-Bomber Group (FBG) had arrived in India recently with four squadrons of P-51As and A-36s (dive-bomber versions of the Mustang), and the decision was made to reorganise the group into three squadrons so the excess P-51As could be reassigned to China. As any prudent commander would do, the CO of the 311th instructed his squadron commanders to make sure that they kept their best Mustangs and sent only the rejects to China.

Soon the surplus Mustangs were flown to Lingling, where a transition school of sorts was set up. Maintenance crews busied themselves painting

with its two-stage supercharger, was the same engine that gave the Spitfire its high service ceiling.

When tests of a Merlin-powered Mustang proved successful, US automobile manufacturer Packard was brought on board to manufacture the British engine under license in America for a new version of the NA-73, designated the P-51B. Another important improvement built into the B-model was the addition of a fuel tank behind the pilot's seat.

Now the Mustang was a world-beater, with speed, manoeuvrability, altitude and range second to none. Built by the thousands, Merlin-powered P-51s fought on virtually every front from late 1943

through to the end of the war. In 1944, NAA redesigned the fuselage with a streamlined bubble canopy to improve visibility from the cockpit and fitted a more powerful Merlin engine to produce the P-51D. The latter variant would be produced in greater numbers than any other model of the Mustang, with 6502 built in NAA's Los Angeles factory and 1454 built in Dallas, Texas. A similar version, the P-51K, was fitted with a different propeller.

In addition, photo-reconnaissance versions of various models of the Mustang were designated as F-6s. A lightweight version of the fighter (P-51H) was introduced after the war had ended.

sharksmouths on the aeroplanes, although the smooth line of the P-51A's lower cowling did not lend itself particularly well to the now-famous group marking.

As time permitted, pilots of the 76th came from Hengyang and Suichuan (a forward base south of Hengyang where a detachment was stationed) to check out in their new fighters.

The Mustangs were in short supply, and there was no assurance that replacements would be available any time soon. With this in mind, Col Vincent was leery of basing the new aeroplanes in Hengyang, where they would face greatest exposure to enemy air attack. Instead, he instructed the 75th and 76th FSs to trade places so the P-51As could be stationed at Kweilin – a little farther out of harm's way. The 75th FS flew its P-40s to Hengyang to join the 16th FS on 18 November, and the 76th FS joined the 74th FS at Kweilin. Except for a detachment of eight P-40s based at Suichuan under the command of Capt John S Stewart, the 76th turned

F-6C '599' of the 118th TRS displays the unit's distinctive black lightning markings to good effect. Note the camera port in the lower rear of the fuselage. The squadron was initially assigned numbers '551-600', but it switched to '151-199' in 1945 (*Henry Davis*)

Lt John Celani, foreground, and Capt John Stewart (in '122') strap into their P-51As at Kweilin in late 1943. The 76th FS initially received 15 Mustangs, and the pilots immediately appreciated the increases in speed and range that the aircraft gave them over the P-40 (*Tom Raleigh*)

over its remaining P-40s to the 16th FS. The Lightnings of the 449th FS stayed at Lingling.

THANKSGIVING DAY RAID ON FORMOSA

Col Hill had flown from Kunming to Kweilin, now site of the 23rd FG headquarters, on 4 November 1943, where he assumed command of the group from Lt Col Bonawitz, who in turn stayed on as group executive officer. The two of them, along with Col Vincent, soon cooked up a plan to mount a surprise attack against Shinchiku airfield on the island of Formosa (now Taiwan), which Col Bruce Holloway had scouted several months earlier in a daring solo reconnaissance mission.

Heavy dust at Kweilin was blamed for two accidents by the 74th FS on 4 November 1943. Three P-40s were destroyed in a take-off incident while scrambling for an air raid alert, and one more was wrecked when the aeroplanes came back in to land. 'The boys sure needed a bracer after this fiasco', the squadron historian noted (*Leon Klesman*)

Hill recalled years later how the Shinchiku mission developed;

'It was something that was absolutely secret. Bruce Holloway had done some recce over there. I saw Bruce when I was coming in, and he was on his way back to the States. He told me, "Man, 'Tex', they've got a lot of aeroplanes over there if you can just get to them". Casey Vincent and I dreamed up a way to do it with what we had. We took everything in China to make that trip.'

The Forward Echelon dispatched an F-5A photo-reconnaissance aircraft from Suichuan on 24 November to check out the Japanese airfield at Shinchiku. When the aeroplane arrived over Formosa, its pilot turned onto his photo run, took his pictures and ran for home. The F-5s had been taking pictures over Formosa for several months, but this trip was different. Vincent and Hill had put together a strike force consisting of 14 B-25s, eight P-38s and eight P-51As. If the photos showed sufficient enemy aircraft on Shinchiku to warrant an attack, the mission would go the very next day – even if it was Thanksgiving Day.

The cameras in the F-5 were quickly unloaded after it landed at Suichuan, and the film was processed there. The photographs revealed Japanese aircraft by the dozens parked on the big airfield. In fact Hill recalled the count of 100 bombers and 112 fighters parked all over the place. The mission was on.

At Kweilin, eight P-51A pilots from the 76th FS were alerted immediately for a 1400 hrs flight to Suichuan. They did not know where they would be going from Suichuan, but they knew something big was up when they were issued 'Mae West' life preservers – the first they had seen since arriving in China. Col Hill led the Mustangs off at 1415 hrs, and they arrived at Suichuan 90 minutes later. That same afternoon, P-38s from Lingling and B-25s from Kweilin also flew to Suichuan. The pilots went to bed early because reveille was scheduled for 0400 hrs on Thanksgiving Day.

The 76th FS learned of its target at an extensive briefing held at 0830 hrs on Thanksgiving morning. The route to Shinchiku would take the Mustang pilots 424 miles out and about the same distance back, plus whatever manoeuvring might be necessary during the attack itself, when the likelihood of engagement by the JAAF was high. Nearly 100 miles each way would be over the water of the Formosa Strait. Upon leaving Suichuan, the aeroplanes would take an initial heading northeast, as if they were going to Hankow, and then turn southeast toward the northern end of Formosa. They were to approach the island at low level to avoid radar detection, climb to 1000 ft just southwest of Shinchiku and proceed with the attack from there.

The P-38s would provide top cover, with the Mustangs staying close to the B-25s. Six of the bombers were from the 2nd BS of the Chinese-American Composite Wing, which had just arrived in China – this was the unit's first combat mission. The other eight B-25s were from the veteran 11th BS.

According to the plan, the P-38s would escort the B-25s directly to the target, engage any interceptors, and then strafe the airfield. The B-25s would follow them in and drop parachute-retarded fragmentation bomb clusters on one side of the field, while P-51s strafed the other side, as well as the dispersal areas. If any fighters went down in the strait on the way

Six-victory ace Maj J M 'Willie' Williams commanded the 76th FS from October through to late December 1943, when he was sent to India to serve as an instructor prior to returning to the US (*John Stewart*)

Japanese bombers burn on the ramp at Shinchiku airfield, Formosa, on Thanksgiving Day 1943. Col 'Tex' Hill led the escorts on this long-range raid in a 76th FS P-51A, scoring an aerial victory and a ground kill whilst over Formosa (*Bob Colbert*)

home, the last B-25 was to circle back and drop a life raft to the pilot. The airmen also had the name of a missionary to contact in a coastal town south of Foochow should they go down over the Chinese mainland near the coast.

Col Hill would be the mission leader, as well as the leader of the P-51 escorts. Capt John Stewart, Suichuan detachment commander, convinced junior P-51 pilot in the formation Lt Joe Hiner to give up his seat so Stewart could go. The other Mustang pilots involved in the mission were Capts J M 'Willie' Williams and Lee Manbeck, and Lts Donald Hedrick, Bob Colbert, Richard Olney and Dale Bell.

Take-offs began at 0930 hrs, and they had to be done in single file because of soggy field conditions. The last aeroplane was off by 1000 hrs, and the pilots settled down for their long run to the target. Capt Manbeck had not gone far when he encountered a problem with his hydraulic system and became the only pilot to abort the mission. The 29-aeroplane formation stuck closely to its flight plan, and the navigation was absolutely accurate. The Americans crossed the coast of Formosa at about noon and headed north toward their target.

Capt John S Stewart, shown here in mid-1943, replaced Willie Williams as commander of the 76th FS and went on to become its top-scoring ace with nine confirmed victories by the time he left China in May 1944 after two years of overseas service (*Dick Templeton*)

A few moments later someone called in a twin-engined enemy aircraft approaching down the coastline. Col Hill despatched a flight of the P-38s to go after it, and 1Lt Robert Schultz quickly shot the aeroplane down. The Lightning flight was returning to its station when Hill spotted some enemy fighters taking off from the airfield ahead. A few seconds later, the P-38s found themselves in a fighter pilot's dream position when they saw a string of enemy bombers strung out low and slow in the landing pattern for their air base. A short but decisive battle ensued.

The P-38s had a field day, destroying 11 Japanese bombers while the B-25s swept across Shinchiku. On the ground, Japanese crewmen ran for their lives as the B-25s dropped their deadly 'frag' bomb clusters. Meanwhile, Col Hill's Mustangs engaged a few Ki-43 'Oscars' that managed to get airborne. Hill shot down one that 'chandelled' in front of him while it tried to get on the tail of the last B-25. Lt Bell sent another fighter down in flames a few seconds later. Then Hill led his P-51s in on a strafing run, and the flight destroyed several more aircraft on the ground. The B-25s and P-38s also did considerable damage to aircraft and facilities on the airfield.

Not a single USAAF aircraft was lost in return, although two of the P-51 pilots had frightening moments. Ironically, the first was Capt Stewart, who had never previously flown a Mustang prior to embarking on this mission. He dropped his external wing tanks just before going down on his strafing pass but forgot to turn on the switch to his internal fuel tanks. The Mustang's engine died immediately, leaving it to glide silently across the airfield while Stewart scrambled frantically to find the fuel switch. He got the engine restarted just in time to take aim at a bomber parked on the field's edge and fire a burst that blew it up.

Col Hill had the second scare as he was pulling up from his strafing pass. He was just forming up for the flight home when an explosion rocked his Mustang. Hill's heart jumped, and he shot a glance over his shoulder to try to spot the enemy fighter that must surely be behind him. Nothing was there, however, leaving him to surmise that a round of ammunition had cooked off in one of his hot wing guns. No harm was done, except perhaps to his nerves, and Hill led the formation back to Suichuan without further excitement.

'It was a risky operation', 'Tex' Hill told the author many years later. 'We could have easily lost everybody. Instead, we pulled off a perfect mission'.

A photo-reconnaissance Lightning arrived over Shinchiku at high altitude about 15 minutes after the attackers had departed and took pictures of the carnage below. Those images, in addition to some taken from the B-25s during the attack, helped to confirm the following claims by the P-51 pilots – Hill, one confirmed in the air plus one confirmed and one probable on the ground; Williams, one confirmed and one damaged on the ground; Stewart, one confirmed on the ground; Colbert, one confirmed on the ground; and Hedrick, one probable and one damaged on the ground. The only damage sustained by the Mustangs occurred when Lt Rick Olney made a rough landing at Suichuan and badly damaged the propeller on his aeroplane. The P-51As returned to Kweilin the next day.

Accolades poured in to Col Vincent's office in Kweilin over the next few days from as far away as India. The mission was deemed to have been a complete success, for not only had it inflicted specific damage on Japanese

Lt Lyndon R 'Deacon' Lewis of the 75th FS prepares for a mission in his P-40K '169' *Deacon's SAD SACK*. Lewis scored two confirmed aerial victories, one probable and two damaged in action from May through to December 1943. The significance of the cut-off drop tank is unknown (*Lyndon Lewis*)

aircraft and installations at Shinchiku, it also had strategic value. No longer could the Japanese assume that Formosa was out of reach from an enemy air attack. The JAAF would have to bolster its air defences on the island, using aircraft and men badly needed to oppose Allied advances in the South Pacific.

DEFENDING THE RICE BOWL

On 13 November, units of the Japanese 11th Army had moved out of their camps in the Hankow area and headed west toward the Chinese-held city of Changteh (Changde), on the far side of Tungting Lake. The primary goal of this manoeuvre was to relieve Chinese farmers in the rice-rich area of their crops, which were needed to feed Japanese soldiers elsewhere. The 23rd FG squadrons in east China responded ferociously, raining down a torrent of bombs and bullets on the enemy advance, but by 1 December the Japanese had surrounded Changteh and held it under siege. At this point the P-40 pilots converted their Warhawks into transports, filling belly tanks with ammunition and food that they dropped to the Chinese troops defending the city.

The first aerial battle over Changteh took place on 4 December, when pilots of the 74th and 75th FSs fought off Ki-44 'Tojos' attempting to attack the B-25s they were escorting. More clashes occurred as the month progressed, and on 12 December the Japanese struck back with a series of raids on Hengyang. After the first formation of 'Tojos' and 'Oscars' broke off an engagement over Hengyang and headed for their base at Nanchang that day, Capt Lynn F Jones of the 74th FS gave chase at the head of a fresh flight of P-40s. Jones caught the enemy formation by surprise near Nanchang and shot down an 'Oscar' for his fifth victory.

Also on 12 December a replacement pilot with the 75th FS recorded one of the more unusual aerial victories of the China air war. Flying in a wingman slot, 2Lt Donald S Lopez lost sight of his flight leader in the haze

P-51A '114' (43-6298) bellied in at Kweilin on 18 December 1943 with Lt John Celani at the controls, the pilot having clipped the wing of a wrecked B-25 while taking off on a practice flight. Note the mechanics removing the canopy. These were in short supply in China, and could be used as replacement items on another aeroplane (*Tom Raleigh*)

The 76th FS sent 16 P-40s and P-51s, along with P-40s from the 74th and 16th FSs, as escorts for B-24s targeting Canton on 23 December 1943. Lt Richard Perkins made it back to Kweilin, but had to belly-land P-40K '102' there. Note the dark border (probably red) on the fighter's national insignia (*Victor Gelhausen*)

after their first pass at a formation of 'Oscars'. Lopez then spotted a Ki-43 chasing another P-40 and began closing in on it from behind. The 'Oscar' pilot spotted Lopez and whipped around in a tight turn to make a head-on pass. Both pilots opened fire, and Lopez could see his bullets hitting home, but by then the two aeroplanes were practically on top of each other. The Japanese pilot veered sharply to his right, but the left wings of the two fighters struck each other. Lopez felt a jolt and looked back to see the wing of the 'Oscar' separate from the fuselage, sending it whirling down in a crazy dive. The P-40's wing was mangled but intact, and Lopez managed to land his aeroplane without incident at Hengyang. Lopez's victory was the first of five he would score in China.

In all, 23rd FG pilots were credited with 16 confirmed victories on 12 December.

The 76th FS, under newly appointed commanding officer Capt John S Stewart, moved its P-51As from Kweilin to the forward base at Suichuan, on the Kan River in south Kiangsi Province, on 26 December 1943. Japanese intelligence was apparently very good in this area because the JAAF's 3rd Air Division launched an attack on the base from Canton the very next morning.

Seven P-51As and seven P-40s scrambled at 1130 hrs on word from the warning net that an attack was on the way. At about 1145 hrs, six Ki-48 'Lily' bombers made a bombing run over the base from south to north at 1500 ft, destroying a B-25 in a revetment plus the 76th FS alert shack. Meanwhile, Capt Stewart led his mixed formation in a bounce of the escorting Ki-43s of the 11th and 25th Sentais from above at 12,000 ft over the base.

A tremendous fight ensued, and all but one of Stewart's pilots would subsequently submit claims for the fight, including five Ki-43s destroyed. This was an unusually accurate tally, as the 25th Sentai lost three aircraft and the 11th Sentai lost one. Among the Japanese pilots killed was Capt Nakakazu Ozaki, commander of the 2nd Chutai/25th Sentai and a

Technically, the Chinese Army was in charge of ground defence for the airfields, but that did not stop the 74th FS from mounting this 0.50-cal machine gun in a pit at Kweilin. Here, Sgt Leon Klesman is seen getting used to the feel of the big gun, which was salvaged from a written-off P-40 (*Leon Klesman*)

19-victory ace. He crashed about ten kilometres southwest of Suichuan. The only 76th aircraft lost was Lt Robert Schaeffer's P-40K No 112. He was shot up during the initial bounce but managed to belly-land his aeroplane nearby and was unhurt.

76th FS pilots claimed four more victories when Japanese fighters attacked Suichuan on 30 December, thus boosting the 23rd FG's total for the month to a new group record of 41 confirmed kills during the course of 962 sorties.

This total did not include a victory credited to 76th FS crew chief SSgt George Spencer on 30 December. Spencer was manning a water-cooled 0.50-cal machine gun in a pit at the southern end of the Suichuan airfield when a strafing Ki-43 flew over him and pulled up in a steep dive to reverse direction for another pass. Spencer got a good lead on the aeroplane and fired 125 rounds in two bursts before his gun jammed. Although he did not see his rounds inflict any damage on the fighter, a group of mechanics taking shelter at the northern end of the field saw the 'Oscar' nose into the ground and blow up. SSgt Spencer was subsequently awarded a Silver Star for this action.

One other notable event took place at the end of 1943 when the Fourteenth Air Force reorganised its combat forces geographically to operate under the command of individual wings. The 23rd FG and the 11th BS were assigned to the 68th Composite Wing (CW), which would operate in eastern China under the command of none other than Col Casey Vincent.

1944 started quietly for the 23rd FG as bad weather shut down flying in eastern China for a week. Maintenance crews used the time to install new Bendix radio compasses in some of the unit's fighters. These devices were navigational aids that allowed pilots to take a 'fix' from a ground transmitter to determine their location and the proper heading back to base. The compasses, like everything else in China, were in short supply, so initially they were fitted only to aeroplanes assigned to squadron leaders and flight commanders. Bendix radio compasses were installed in existing group aircraft through to April, by which time new fighters had begun to arrive in China with compasses already fitted.

Another maintenance issue concerned the tyres fitted to new P-40Ns that began arriving in-theatre in December 1943. The gravel runways in China were notoriously hard on tyres, and the Fourteenth Air Force had worked hard to build up a supply of replacement rubber for its Warhawks. However, the P-40N-5 and later models were fitted with smaller wheels and tyres than the earlier P-40s in an effort to reduce overall weight, and there were no replacement tyres available for them. In some cases, crew chiefs backdated the landing gears of their P-40Ns with bigger wheels salvaged from older fighters so they would be able to replace the tyres when they wore out.

Although the 23rd FG had by now become famous for its prowess in air-to-air combat, by 1944 the unit was primarily involved in fighter-bomber operations aimed at harassing the enemy's long, and vulnerable, lines of communication. River, rail and highway traffic were common targets, along with Japanese-held airfields, dock facilities, bridges and troop concentrations.

The first mission of 1944 was a sweep by nine P-40s of the 75th FS on 9 January. Covering 50 miles of the Yangtze River from Hankow eastward to Kiukiang, the pilots involved shot up six steamboats and numerous smaller craft, causing an estimated 30 to 40 casualties. All of the 'Sharks' returned safely to Hengyang, thus completing the 75th's most successful mission of the month.

The Mustangs at Suichuan were in action the following day when Capt Stewart led eight 76th FS P-51As to Kienchang to attack a railway bridge. This first attempt at dive-bombing with the Mustangs was disappointing,

Tom Raleigh was a 'tech rep' from the Allison Division of General Motors, and he is seen here posing with Capt John Stewart's P-51A '122' (43-6303) in early 1944 at Suichuan. Named for Stewart's wife, Lynn, the aeroplane displays its pilot's full score of nine victory flags. It has also been fitted with a direction finding loop on the fuselage spine (*Tom Raleigh*)

as two bombs hit the tracks south of the bridge, but not one of the 14 remaining bombs hit the bridge itself. Soon, however, the 76th FS pilots would get the hang of dive-bombing with their new fighters, and the Mustang would ultimately prove itself to be as fine a dive-bomber as it was a fighter.

Air-to-air combat was sporadic during the first two months of 1944, with the 23rd FG claiming nine Japanese aircraft shot down in seven encounters. The 23rd FG lost two P-40s and one P-51A in aerial combat during this period, plus two more Warhawks that were shot down by enemy ground fire.

The weather also proved a dangerous opponent. On 18 January five pilots left Kunming to ferry new P-40Ns to Kweilin. Leading was Capt Harlyn S Vidovich, a highly experienced pilot in the 74th FS with two confirmed victories to his credit. None of the fighters arrived in Kweilin, and their fate remained a mystery for more than a week before a survivor was located and told his story.

Apparently, the P-40 pilots had become trapped in the clouds and succumbed to vertigo. Two managed to parachute to safety, but Capt Vidovich, 1Lt Lawrence W Smith and 2Lt Walter C Washer were killed. It was a powerful reminder of the hazards that threatened fighter pilots in China every time they left the ground.

March brought two exciting developments, though only one would prove successful. After a short period of training at Kweilin, the 74th FS flew the first combat mission employing aerial M-9 rockets in China on 3 March. Carried in long bazooka-like tubes under the wings of a P-40, the early rockets packed a strong punch but were not considered particularly accurate, plus the tubes were a tremendous drag on the performance of the

P-40K '36' of the 74th FS, assigned to Lt Fred Meyer, came to rest in a ditch at Kweilin in early 1944. Note the squadron's red fuselage band and the pin-up artwork of a girl in a bathing suit wearing a big hat on the rudder. This artwork was applied to both sides of the rudder (*Leon Klesman*)

aircraft. John W. Wheeler, a pilot in the 74th FS during this period, had this to say about the rockets;

'We thought it was the first time rockets had been used in combat by fighter planes. They were triple tubes, about six inches (in) diameter, and we carried one cluster under each wing. They made a nice explosion when they hit, but I only used them on one mission and they petered out pretty quickly. I think it was hard to get an accurate shot. They were an awful drag, too, and we seldom dropped belly tanks or bazooka tubes except in emergency because everything was too hard to replace.'

After this disappointing start, rocket use would increase slowly as accuracy of the weapons improved and supplies became more reliable. A more positive development, at least for the 76th FS, was the arrival of the first five P-51Bs at Kunming. These new Merlin-powered Mustangs, which had a substantial performance edge over every other fighter type flying in the Far East at that time, were delivered to the 76th FS at Suichuan on 14 March after having been modified by the air service group at Kunming. Shortages of spare parts and tools would hamper the combat introduction of the new Mustangs, but over the next eight months they would displace the P-40 as the standard fighter of the 23rd FG.

The arrival of spring did not bring an increase in operations, as the 23rd FG recorded just 59 offensive sorties and no enemy aircraft claimed in the air or on the ground during April. This period of relative quiet gave the unit a chance to catch its breath and build up its strength; the number of aircraft assigned to the 23rd FG grew from just 53 at the beginning of the year to 75 in April. That was fortunate, because the 23rd FG would need all the strength it could muster in the months to come.

The first Merlin-powered P-51B Mustangs, instantly recognisable by their four-bladed propellers, arrived in China in March 1944 as replacements for the tired P-51As of the 76th FS. Here, one of the new fighters makes a low pass over an airfield while on an early test hop (*Ray Crowell*)

BATTLING *ICHI-GO*

The war in the Pacific was going badly for the Japanese by the spring of 1944. In the CBI, long-ranging sweeps over the South China Sea by Fourteenth Air Force bombers, plus attacks by American submarines, were seriously disrupting Japanese shipments of oil and ore from Southeast Asia to the home islands. The best units of the Chinese Army, meanwhile, were adding strength to the Allied ground campaign in northern Burma.

The Japanese High Command decided its best course of action would be to mount a massive ground campaign that would conquer all of southern China and possibly force Chiang Kai-shek out of the war. The offensive, named *Ichi-Go* ('Number One') was designed to capture the Fourteenth Air Force's pesky eastern airbases and also to provide the Japanese with a railway link for hauling war materials all the way from Indochina through Hankow and on to Peking (Beijing), Korea and Manchuria. It nearly succeeded.

Ichi-Go kicked off in April 1944 with a drive south from the Yellow River into Honan Province in an attempt to complete the railway connection between Hankow and Peking. The Fourteenth Air Force responded by sending the newly arrived 3rd FG of the Chinese-American Combat Wing (CACW) north to oppose the Japanese advance. Soon the 5th FG CACW would move to Chihkiang, leaving the 23rd FG to hold

Col 'Tex' Hill, CO of the 23rd FG, took one of the first P-51Bs (43-12405) as his personal aircraft and named it *BULLFROG I*. Assigned for service to the 74th FS, it carried the tail number '11' and also sported a propeller spinner striped in red, white and blue. The identity of the crewman standing on the fighter's wing in this photograph is unknown (*Leon Klesman*)

the line in the east. This phase of the advance had little impact on the 23rd FG because the action was taking place several hundred miles north of its bases. The second phase of *Ichi-Go*, expected to start at any time, would work its way down the Hsiang River valley from Hankow toward the 23rd FG bases. As soon as the enemy's battle plan became apparent, Col Casey Vincent began planning how his 68th CW would react.

After being delayed for several days by bad weather, Vincent sent a force of 54 fighters and bombers to the Hankow area on 6 May 1944 with the intention of destroying Japanese supplies and equipment before they could be employed in the second phase of the advance. Col Tex Hill would lead the fighter escort, which consisted of 16 P-51Bs from the 76th FS and P-38s of the 449th FS out of Lingling and P-40s of the 75th FS from Hengyang, which would join up en route to the target.

The big formation managed to make its way toward Hankow, despite being hampered by heavy haze and scattered clouds. About ten minutes short of the target, which was a supply depot near the main Hankow airfield, several Ki-43s popped out of the clouds and made a head-on pass on a flight of Mustangs led by Maj Charles E Griffith. The fighters tangled for a few moments and the P-51s got the worst of it, but they managed to keep the 'Oscars' away from the bombers, which hit the target successfully. Lt Glen Beneda of the 76th FS was shot down (the first combat loss of a P-51B in China), but he baled out successfully and returned to the squadron two months later.

The P-38s also engaged some Ki-43s, but the only kill credited to an American pilot went to Col Hill. This was the last victory of his illustrious combat career, giving him a total of 14.75 victories. This clearly made him the highest scoring ace among active Fourteenth Air Force pilots that were active at that time.

Action picked up for the 23rd FG over the coming week, although the 74th FS at Kweilin had to wait until June to engage JAAF aircraft once again. The Japanese sent several strong missions into the Suichuan area on 11 and 12 May that were opposed by a detachment of the 76th FS flying P-40s and P-51s. By the afternoon of the 13th, only three P-51s were

Patsy was a P-40N-1 of the 75th FS, and it is seen here riddled with holes from a fragmentation bomb following a night attack by the JAAF on Hengyang on 3 May 1944. Note also that the fighter's drop tank has been shattered and its tyres punctured (*H L Kirkpatrick*)

airworthy enough to be scrambled when a big formation of enemy raiders again approached the base. Capt Lester Murray led the intercept, but just as he reached the Japanese bombers his engine began coughing white smoke from its exhausts. Thinking he had been hit, Murray dived out of the fight and made an emergency landing. Lt Charles Gibson also tried to close on the bombers, but the Ki-43 escorts cut him off and he spent a very busy few minutes before he was able to evade them.

The only P-51 pilot who managed to attack the bombers was Lt Wendell Stoneham. He caught them flying north after they had made their bombing runs over the base, and he dived on the trailing flight of five Ki-48s. The bombers closed up in a tight formation so their top gunners could concentrate their return fire on the approaching Mustang, but Stoneham ducked below their line of sight and made a climbing pass from beneath the last bomber on the left. His first burst hit the aeroplane's left engine, and then he hit it in the fuselage. The Ki-48 quickly began to burn, and it fell out of formation trailing a long plume of smoke. When the bomber crashed, the smoke from its explosion could be seen from the airfield. Stoneham made two more attacks, setting a second bomber on fire (which he claimed as a probable) and damaging a third.

Maj Charles E Griffith, commander of the 76th FS (hence the squadron patch on his flight jacket), led his squadron on a successful escort mission to Hankow on 6 May 1944. Griffith went on to score three aerial victories, but sadly was killed in a flying accident in December 1944 at Luliang (*Don Scott*)

By this time, however, the damage had been done at Suichuan. The Japanese bombs had destroyed three P-38s and damaged three B-25s and three P-40s.

With the base's fuel supply nearly exhausted, Col Vincent had little choice but to pull his remaining B-25s out of there that same day. Bad weather then set in, and Suichuan remained quiet for the rest of May.

At Hengyang, the 75th FS flew 11 offensive missions – ground attack and bomber escort – plus 15 local alerts during the first 13 days of the month. Now led by Maj Philip C Loofbourrow, the 75th FS finally got a crack at the JAAF after almost two months without a claim when the squadron flew an early morning escort mission to Yochow (Yueyang) on 14 May. Eight P-40s covered the B-25s as they made their bombing runs and then dropped down to strafe a long convoy of trucks, leaving them thoroughly riddled. While climbing out after his strafing pass, one of the Warhawk pilots called out 12 to 14 Ki-43s heading toward the P-40s.

Loofbourrow turned his formation into the attack, and a furious

Maj Philip C Loofbourrow (left) commanded the 75th FS at the start of the *Ichi-Go* offensive, and was subsequently transferred to 23rd FG headquarters, where he followed 'Tex' Hill as group commander on 15 October 1944. With him is Lt Joshua D 'Chief' Sanford, who was also a pilot with the 75th FS (*Everett Hyatt*)

fight ensued. Lts James Vurgaropulos and James Folmar each scored single confirmed kills, and probables were credited to Capt John Long and Lt Francis Armstrong. Seven damaged claims also were filed. The only P-40 to suffer any damage was Maj Loofbourrow's, which was hit in the left stabiliser and fuselage. The major suffered superficial flesh wounds on an arm and leg but returned safely to Hengyang with the rest of the 'Sharks'. 75th FS flight surgeon Maj Laughlin soon had Loofbourrow patched up, and the major led another mission that afternoon.

The 75th FS had another scrap three days later, scoring one victory, four probables and seven damaged, while having two P-40s badly shot up. On that same day, the Japanese army completed its operation in Honan Province to link the Peking-Hankow railway line, and on 26 May the main phase of *Ichi-Go* began. The Japanese Eleventh Army, with some 60,000 assault troops in a force totalling near 250,000, crossed the Yangtze River near Yochow and headed south toward Changsha. Chinese resistance was light at first, but it stiffened as the Japanese approached the city, where Gen Hsueh Yueh was in command of nearly 150,000 defenders.

The pace and profile of missions flown by the 23rd FG changed immediately. Now, in addition to defending their bases and striking at enemy supply lines, the pilots would begin making attacks on the Japanese advance itself. Using bombs, rockets and gunfire, they struck at troop concentrations, tanks and artillery at the front, as well as anything moving along the Japanese lines of communication and transport. Trucks, trains and riverboats were favoured targets, along with bridges and marshalling yards.

JAAF air activity was increasing as well, and the 75th FS lost two pilots killed during a dogfight over the enemy's forward airfield at Kingmen on the first day of the offensive. In all, the 75th FS lost seven P-40s between 26 and 29 May, leaving Hengyang so short of fighter defence

that Col Vincent flew the 76th FS in from Suichuan on 31 May to help bolster the badly shaken 75th. Phil Loofbourrow recalled this period in a letter to the author;

'The majority of our activity in the spring and summer of 1944 was against Japanese ground forces, and Japanese infantrymen shot down more of our aeroplanes than Japanese fighter pilots. For this type of activity, the P-40 probably did better than the P-51 Mustang because the rear-mounted radiator in the latter fighter gave the rifleman a vulnerable target going away from him. Anyone trying to hit the radiator in the P-40 had to stand up and face six 0.50-cal machine guns coming at him. Against fighters, of course, the P-51 was superior because it had about a 100 mph advantage in speed.'

Col Vincent continued shuffling his fighter squadrons to keep his freshest units in the fight. He moved the 74th FS up to Hengyang on 3 June and transferred the P-51Bs of the 76th FS to Lingling. By this time the 75th was nearly out of aircraft, so it followed the 76th to Lingling a few days later. Now the 74th FS was on point at Hengyang, and its new commander, Maj Arthur Cruikshank, intended to make the most of it. Cruikshank had been one of the original 74th FS pilots, and he had become the squadron's first ace in August 1943 prior to returning to the US. Now he was back in China for a second combat tour, and looking to run up his score. By the end of June he had scored two more victories, been shot down twice and then pulled back out of combat.

Chinese forces held the city of Changsha for several weeks, but when it fell Hengyang was left exposed. Col Vincent ordered the 68th CW to abandon its Hengyang base on 16 June, leaving Lingling and Kweilin as the primary airfields available to the 23rd FG. On the plus side, the Chinese defence had stiffened again as the enemy approached Hengyang. At Hengshan, 25 miles north of the city, the defenders held a strong position and were refusing to yield.

P-51B '101' displays typical markings of the 76th FS in the spring-summer of 1944 as it has its guns bore-sighted at Suichuan. The spinner is light blue. The squadron soon stopped applying the sharksmouth to its Mustangs, as the nose shape did not suit the markings particularly well (*Ivan Ball*)

2Lt Don Lopez's P-40N '194' of the 75th FS got a mouthful of aluminium when a P-51 taxied into it at Yang Tong airfield, Kweilin, on 12 June 1944. The tough P-40 suffered only superficial damage to its cowling, which Lopez recalled was replaced with an unmarked 'bathtub', leaving him a 'toothless tiger' until it was painted several weeks later (*Leon Klesman*)

From 17 through to 25 June, the 68th CW threw the full weight of its firepower into supporting the Chinese at Hengshan. The weather was awful, with a low overcast restricting visibility, but mission after mission went out anyway. The majority of these strikes were river sweeps designed to catch the Japanese moving men and supplies along the Hsiang River to support their frontline troops. The pilots of the 23rd FG flew 538 sorties in nine days and lost just one aircraft – Lt David Rust of the 75th FS experienced engine failure in his P-40N and had to make a belly landing ten miles north of Lingling.

The bad weather was a factor in the 23rd FG's low loss rate because Japanese fighters at Hankow were having more trouble reaching the frontline area than the Americans were. And when they did make contact with the Warhawks and Mustangs, the Japanese usually suffered yet more losses. The 76th FS scored three victories without loss on 17 and 18 June. The next contact did not come until 25 June, when Maj Cruikshank led a mixed formation from the 74th and 75th out of Lingling on an offensive sweep along the river north of Hengyang and scored two of the three victories claimed when the P-40s encountered a flight of Japanese dive-bombers with fighter escort.

Also in June 1944, a fourth squadron joined the 23rd FG at Kweilin in the form of the 118th Tactical Reconnaissance Squadron (TRS), commanded by Maj Edward O McComas. The 118th TRS initially flew P-40Ns equipped with aerial cameras as well as guns. These would give way to P-51B/Ds and F-6 Mustangs later in the year. The 118th TRS was a pre-war National Guard unit from Connecticut with highly trained pilots and an aggressive commander. It wasted no time in making their presence felt, flying 64 sorties by the end of June, and by October the unit would boast of its first ace, Capt Oran S Watts.

Lt Stephen J Bonner Jr, who was a five-victory ace with the 76th FS, poses in his P-51B (43-7028) in mid-1944. Unfortunately, the tail number and other possible markings worn by this aeroplane remain unknown (*Steve Bonner*)

The 118th TRS joined the 23rd FG in June 1944 at Kweilin. It initially flew P-40Ns equipped with aerial cameras as well as guns, and Lt Henry F Davis Jr was one of its most successful pilots, scoring three confirmed victories by October 1944 (*Henry Davis*)

With the addition of the new squadron, the 23rd FG began July with 51 aircraft, 182 commissioned officers and 682 enlisted men. The group would lose four fighters in aerial combat during the month, plus 20 others to ground fire, accidents and other causes. One pilot, Lt Richard Mullineaux of the 74th FS, was killed on a strafing mission and another was taken prisoner. On the positive side of the ledger, the 23rd FG was credited with 27 aerial victories, of which Lt James Folmar of the 75th FS claimed four. The group also claimed a total of five aircraft destroyed on the ground too.

The 74th FS began using Kanchow intermittently in July, and it would move there permanently in early September under the command of grey-haired Maj John C 'Pappy' Herbst. Legend held that Herbst had downed a German aeroplane over Europe while flying with the Royal Canadian Air Force in 1941, and his performance since arriving in China in June seemed to support it.

The group's most successful encounter with enemy aircraft came on 15 July when P-40Ns of the 74th FS took on Ki-43-IIs of the 48th Sentai and Ki-44s of the 9th Sentai near the airfield at Siangtan. 74th FS narrative from flight leaders involved in the action read as follows;

'The 74th FS sent seven P-40s led by Capt John C Herbst, squadron commander, (from Kweilin) to stage out of Namyung against the Japanese supply line from Tungchang to Tsyungyang. On 14 July they attacked several truck columns and destroyed more than 50 vehicles. Early the next morning they staged out of Suichuan to attack barracks and flak positions near Siangtan. Aircraft in the dive-bombing flight, led by Capt Theodore A Adams, carried a 250-lb bomb under each wing. The trio of

The 118th TRS applied distinctive black lightning markings to its aircraft in the autumn of 1944. Here, a war-weary P-40N squadron hack shows its squadron colours (*Victor Gelhausen*)

top cover, led by Capt Herbst, was loaded with parafrags. The flights approached Siangtan with the top cover at 8000 ft and the dive-bombers at 6000 ft. Capt Adams was to lead two dive-bombers in on the barracks near the airfield, and Lt Virgil A Butler and his wingman were to attack flak positions near the railway trestle north of the city.'

Capt Adams' narrative;

'I had just located the target and peeled off on my dive-bombing run when I noticed a silver aeroplane below and to the right. It had a high, square-tipped wing and a radial engine. I kept an eye on the silver job because I figured I would come back after I bombed and get it. When I got down to about 2000 ft I saw another Jap to my left. I dropped my bombs and went after him. He was turning across my nose, so I turned in behind him. I had built up so much speed in my dive that I closed in a hurry. I started shooting with a 30-degree deflection and closed so fast I had to duck under to keep from hitting the Jap. He was a "Tojo" with elliptical wings and a big radial engine. I saw smoke trail out his engine and then he fell off and hit the ground. I was at about 1200 ft when I pulled out.

'I saw a whole mass of Japs milling around the field at about 1000 ft. There were at least 20 "Tojos" and "Oscars" in a big landing circle going clockwise around the field. I did a steep 180 and came back over the field. I blacked out in the turn and headed into the Jap circle. One "Tojo" started to pull straight up away from the circle. I still had plenty of excess speed so I followed him up in a vertical climb. We were both going straight up when I opened fire. I saw two big plumes of black smoke trail from his cowling and he stalled out. I had to duck again to avoid a collision. I saw him go down smoking like a chimney.

'There was a squirrel cage formation south of the field with eight "Oscars" chasing their tails and edging away from the main fight. My speed was still up, so I broke into the edge of their circle. One tried to dive out so I gave him a 30-degree burst. I missed, and all of a sudden there were four other "Oscars" coming in on me from behind. They were shooting, but their deflection was off – all trailing. I dived a little and another P-40 came scooting by and scattered the Japs. I came back over the field at 500 ft and saw a "Tojo" going west. I overhauled him and took a 45-degree deflection shot and then cut it down to 20 degrees. I saw pieces fly off his fuselage, but he kept on going.

'By this time one of my coolant lines had cracked and the fluid was boiling out. My gauge was clear over on the peg, so I shoved the nose down and started for the Chinese side of the lines to the southwest. Two Japs chased me, and I could see four others on the tail of another P-40. The Japs couldn't gain on me, and the coolant saw me home. I found out later that Lt Van Sickle (on detached duty from the 81st FG at Chengtu) had shot an "Oscar" off my tail as I turned into my first "Tojo". I never even knew the Jap was there.'

Lt Butler's narrative;

'I was after some flak positions near the railway trestle north of the field. I made my bomb run and went after the silver, square-winged, Jap. All of a sudden I picked up three Japs on my tail. While I was diving and twisting to get away from them, a "Tojo" loomed up ahead in my sights. He had his flaps and wheels down and was almost dead ahead below me. I lowered my nose and took a good long shot from squarely astern. He

Lt Frederick M Bear of the 74th FS flew P-40N '31' during the spring and summer of 1944. Barely visible over the exhausts is the fighter's fitting nickname, *THE CUB*, but the artwork applied to the aircraft's rudder is indistinguishable (*Leon Klesman*)

looked as though someone had struck a match along his fuselage – just a long, growing flare of flame. He rolled over and crashed, still burning. I kept on diving down to the deck and eventually succeeded in getting away from the other three Japs.'

Capt Herbst's narrative;

'I was leading the top cover at 8000 ft when I heard Capt Adams call, "There is a Jap down here". At the same time I spotted three black fighters coming in toward us. They must have been top cover for whatever was going on below. I turned into them and they turned away. I never did see them again. We dropped our frag bombs and belly tanks and started down. We picked up a terrific speed in that dive – enough to carry us all the way through the fight with an advantage.

'At 3000 ft I saw two black columns rising from two Jap aeroplanes that had already hit the deck. Then I spotted a lot of Japs at about 1000 ft circling clockwise and a couple of P-40s weaving in and out of the circle. There were two dust streamers rising along the runway where two more Japs were taking off. I counted at least 16 "Oscars" and "Tojos" all strung out in the circle apparently following their leader. They made no effort to get away – the Jap fighters just went around and around.

'I started to cut inside the circle, but I had so much speed – about 340 mph – that I had to weave in and out to get shots. It was a real slugging match. We had the speed and altitude on them, and at close range those six 0.50-cals tore them apart. I took a couple of snap shots and missed. The Japs just went round and round – none of their usual tricks, not even steep, tight turns. They seemed to be afraid to do any stunts at such a low altitude. Our boys had been flying on the deck for so long – strafing and dodging hills in bad weather – that nobody thought twice about racking around in vertical banks ten feet off the deck. It was just our meat.

'I spotted an "Oscar" with his wheels down at about 600 ft. I slowed down and came in directly behind him, and a little above. I gave him a two-second burst and he erupted in flames. I saw him crash.

'By that time I had picked up a "Tojo" on my tail, with an "Oscar" behind him. I also could see other smoke columns rising from crashed aeroplanes. The "Tojo" opened fire, but all his shots were trailing. I could out-turn him, but the moment I got ahead the "Oscar" would cut across the circle and cut me off. I flipped over and started turning in the opposite direction. The same thing happened. I was surprised that I could turn inside the "Tojo", but he seemed unwilling to make a tight turn at 500 ft. Finally, I shoved the stick down and dived under the "Oscar" as he cut across to head me off. That cleared my tail, and I looked around.

'There was a P-40 south of the field with a "Tojo" on his tail at 800 ft. The P-40 was diving and the "Tojo" turning into him to get a deflection shot ahead of him. I turned into the "Tojo" from high astern. My first burst was over him, and he saw the tracers. He flipped over and tried to dive out in the opposite direction. That brought him squarely into my sights for a no-deflection shot, and I gave him another burst that nearly burned out my guns. He went down in flames. I then climbed to 500 ft and came back across the field. There were only three Zeros left still circling the base. I went after them, along with about five other P-40s. We made a couple of passes and didn't hit anything. Leaving the field, I saw columns of smoke rising from the ground.'

Herbst went on to score his fourth and fifth victories (both 'Oscars') on 6 August while leading his squadron in a strike against its former base at Hengyang. With the squadron's conversion to Mustangs in September,

Lt John W Wheeler sits in the cockpit of his P-40N '41' during the 74th FS's spell at Kweilin in mid-1944. Wheeler scored his lone aerial victory on 22 November 1944 during a long-range strike against the enemy airfield at Anking (*John Wheeler*)

Herbst's score really began to rise. By the time he left China in early 1945, his 18 victories tied him with Lt Col Charles Older of 23rd FG HQ as top ace in the CBI.

Air operations of the 23rd FG continued to intensify in August. The squadrons spent the first week concentrating on enemy truck convoys that were supplying the siege forces at Hengyang. Casey Vincent recorded in his diary that his aeroplanes had destroyed or badly damaged nearly 300 trucks on the first day of the month alone. Air battles with Japanese fighters continued as well.

The wear and tear on pilots and aircraft during the summer of 1944 was tremendous. Figures from the 75th FS were typical. The squadron began April with 23 P-40s in combat condition, but by 1 June that number was down to 13, and it dropped to 11 on 1 July, before rising slightly in August and September. Likewise, the squadron lost eight pilots between mid-

One of the 75th FS pilots in the thick of the action during the summer and autumn of 1944 was Lt Jesse B Gray. He scored one aerial victory, four probables and five aircraft damaged prior to being killed in a Jeep accident near Luliang in early 1945 while awaiting orders to return home (*John Rosenbaum*)

May and 1 October 1944, compared to just two during the same period in 1943. On the plus side, 75th FS pilots confirmed 35 aerial victories, plus dozens of probable and damaged claims during this period.

The squadron commander, Maj Don Quigley, reached ace status on 5 August while flying a weather reconnaissance mission near Hengyang. First, he spotted six 'Oscars' in formation above him at 12,000 ft. Seconds later he saw six more aeroplanes below him. Quigley climbed into the overcast and then dove through the top cover to attack a single-engined bomber in the lower formation. He blasted it from astern, and the aeroplane crashed near the runway at Hengyang while the 23rd FG's newest ace made good his getaway. Unfortunately, Quigley was shot down by ground fire five days later, and he spent the rest of the conflict as a PoW.

Future 75th FS ace 1Lt Forrest F Parham claimed his first victory on 19 August during an early morning sweep in the Changsha area. Parham, a former flight instructor, was flying on Capt Joe Brown's wing when they encountered enemy aircraft about 20 miles southeast of Yochow. Parham followed as Brown dove in behind a single-engined bomber and shot it down with a short burst. Climbing back up, the P-40s were attacked by 'Oscars'. Brown got behind one of the Ki-43s and shot it down too, while Parham climbed on up to 12,000 ft. There, he saw what he identified as a 'Hamp' 2000 ft below him attacking a P-40. Parham dove onto the tail of the enemy fighter and opened fire. Getting hits, he followed it down to 7000 ft, where he saw the pilot bale out. Parham went on to score five confirmed victories with the 75th FS.

Capt Forrest F 'Pappy' Parham had just scored his fourth confirmed victory when his crew chief, Sgt Bob Perrin, was photographed painting a new victory flag on Parham's P-51C '187' *Little Jeep*. Parham scored his fifth victory to become an ace on 12 November 1944 (*Forrest Parham*)

The Chinese defenders held out at Hengyang for 44 days before the Japanese finally broke the siege on 8 August and took the city. Meanwhile, the long-expected Japanese drive out of Canton had started in July when troops headed west toward Liuchow (Liuzhou), home of the 76th FS. When the latter unit had exhausted the supply of 500-lbs bombs at Liuchow in mid-August, the 76th FS moved to Erh Tong airfield at Kweilin to share space with the 118th TRS. From there, the squadrons could strike at the Japanese advance, which was now steadily bearing down on Lingling.

The Mustangs of the 76th FS paid special attention to road and railway bridges along the line of the Japanese advance. The P-51 was well-suited for dive-bombing bridges because it was easy to trim in a dive, whereas the P-40 had a tendency to roll. Lt Harry Zavakos gained a reputation as the 76th's premier bridge-buster, and he proved to be so adept at this mission that whenever he flew a sortie his flight was given two targets – one for him and one for the three pilots flying with him!

Despite the best efforts of the 23rd FG, Lingling fell on 7 September. This in turn forced the hasty evacuation of Kweilin two days later. From Indochina, other Japanese ground forces began moving northeast to link up with the advance, targeting new Fourteenth Air Force airfields at Nanning and Liuchow.

With the loss of his Hsiang River Valley air bases looming, Brig Gen Chennault had to find new homes for his 68th CW squadrons. But instead of pulling all of them back toward Kunming and Chungking, he looked east to a Chinese-held pocket of territory between Hankow and Canton. There, he had been stockpiling supplies at the Suichuan and Kanchow (Ganzhou) sites for months.

A key element in the success of any fighter group is the dedication and skill of its groundcrews, and the 23rd FG was no exception. These armourers of the 75th FS at Chihkiang lived by the slogan painted above the door behind them – *IF IT'S GOT WINGS, WE CAN MAKE IT FLY*. They are in the front row, from left to right, Boveer, Stivers, Gerber, Hyatt and Cohen, and in the back row, from left to right, Keller, Nash, Pzchozkie, Sutton, Lt Bowen, Taylor, Washburn and Sanders (*Everett Hyatt*)

The bases were too remote to support the operations of all four 23rd FG squadrons, however, so the 74th FS went to Kanchow and the 118th TRS moved to Suichuan after a short stay at Liuchow. From Kweilin, the 75th FS went 140 miles north to Chihkiang, where it would share the base with the 5th FG CACW. The 76th FS first went south to Tanchuk and then pulled back to Liuchow several weeks later.

By the end of the year, the Japanese had completed their transport link, but had fallen short of their goal for *Ichi-Go* because the railway was useless as long as it remained vulnerable to air attack. The Fourteenth Air Force, by maintaining air superiority, saw to it that the line never went into service. Nor were the Japanese able to use the airfields they had captured, except for staging occasional night missions.

A primary focus of 23rd FG operations in 1944 was the interdiction of enemy supply lines. Railway bridges, such as this one near Liuchow, became key targets for dive-bombing (*Abner Hamm*)

Chinese army guards patrol the flightline at Kanchow in late 1944 as P-51Bs of the 74th FS await their next mission. Unit markings at this time consisted of just a two-digit number on the rudder. Note that '29' is fitted with a fin extension (*John Wheeler*)

LONG HAUL TO VICTORY

The autumn of 1944 was a time of transition for the 23rd FG. As the squadrons settled in at their new bases after abandoning Kweilin, group headquarters was doing likewise at Luliang, a field about 50 miles east of Kunming that was intended for heavy bombers. Similarly, the group's familiar sharkmouthed P-40s were rapidly being replaced by new P-51B/C Mustangs. The squadrons also were gaining strength in numbers. The 23rd FG grew from 48 aircraft assigned on 1 September to 105 on 1 October.

With the transition to Mustangs, the squadrons started coming up with new markings. The 118th TRS adorned its aircraft with a distinctive black lightning bolt with yellow trim that ran nearly the length of the fuselage, plus a smaller version around the wing and tail tips and a black band around the propeller spinner, which in some cases was painted yellow. The details of these markings varied from one airframe to the next, but the 118th arguably flew the most attractively marked Mustangs in the whole of the CBI.

The older squadrons soon followed suit. The 74th and 75th FSs, having initially flown P-51s marked only with an individual squadron number on the tail, went with large areas of black paint. The 74th painted its

The 75th FS has just started to apply black tail markings to its Mustangs when this photograph was taken at Chihkiang in late 1944 (*Everett Hyatt*)

aeroplanes from the cockpit forward, scalloped at the back and covering the entire nose. The 75th painted the entire tail black with an angled break across the rear of the fuselage and a parallel black stripe just forward of the break.

The 76th FS had already dropped the sharksmouth from its Mustangs and initially used only a blue propeller spinner to distinguish its Merlin-powered Mustangs. Later, the squadron went to a black-striped spinner and applied a large Indian chief's head in profile – black on natural metal aircraft and white on olive drab machines – on the vertical tail in recognition of its call sign, 'Pontiac'.

As the markings changed, so did the personnel in the squadrons. Pilots had racked up a lot of missions over the summer of 1944, and by October many were reaching the magic number 100, which earned them a ticket home. Even some pilots in the 118th TRS, who had only been in China since June, were completing their tours and returning to the US. This, combined with combat losses, made for a lot of new faces in the squadrons.

Col 'Tex' Hill got orders sending him home on 15 October, ending one of the most legendary combat careers of all the American pilots who flew in China during the war. He was replaced by Lt Col Phil Loofbourrow, former 75th FS commander, who in turn passed the baton to Col Ed Rector at the end of the year. Rector had returned to China for a second tour after serving in the AVG and the 76th FS in 1941-42.

One of the new pilots was Capt Barney Fudge, who was assigned to the 74th FS after spending two years on instructor duty in the US. He described squadron life in a letter written after the war;

'Newcomers were kidded and called "new jokers". We had nice facilities at Kanchow, where about 20 of us lived in each of two buildings with two

Lt Robert L Schaeffer's *JEANNE IV* '103', sporting two victory flags, heads this line-up of blue-nosed 76th FS P-51s at Liuchow in the autumn of 1944. *FAYE* and *JUDY* are next in line (*Don Scott*)

The 76th FS and 118th TRS flew missions from Liuchow until the Japanese ground advance made the base untenable in early November 1944. As had happened previously at Hengyang, Lingling and Kweilin, rail cars were loaded with supplies and equipment for removal to safety farther west before the air base was demolished (*Lyman Martin*)

men to each room. My most vivid memory of that period was that even with the mosquito nets over our beds, we would be awakened when a rat would join us on the bed with only the mosquito net separating us. Our squadron was composed of a great group of young men who got along well and had a good time. I know that I thought I was suffering tremendous hardships at that time, but now I can only think of the good fellowship and fun.'

Combat operations dropped off by nearly a third in October, due largely to the onset of bad weather at mid-month. The 74th FS was pursuing guerilla tactics at Kanchow, hitting enemy targets deeper in eastern China than ever before. The 76th and 118th, at Liuchow, were busy battling Japanese troops advancing on the base from two directions. When Liuchow fell the following month, the Japanese had a clear path past the Fourteenth Air Force base at Nanning and on into Indochina. The 75th FS spent a fairly quiet October in Chihkiang.

Nevertheless, losses remained high at 28 aircraft, including three P-51s and seven P-40Ns of the 76th FS that went down between Liuchow and Luliang when their ferry flights became trapped in storms. On the plus side, 23rd FG pilots accounted for 16 Japanese aircraft destroyed in the air and 13 more on the ground during the month.

The biggest mission of the month – indeed one of the biggest missions flown by the Fourteenth Air Force to date – occurred on 16 October, when the 76th FS and 118th TRS provided escort for a strike by B-24s and B-25s on Hong Kong.

Flying that day was Lt H L Kirkpatrick, a 75th FS pilot on temporary duty with the 76th. This is his account of the operation;

'The mission was very dicey for the P-40s – I was flying one of them – as we were at the limit of our range, and an early drop of the external tank meant that you would not get home. The B-24s were jumped by Zeros inbound to the target, so a fight was already underway when we arrived. The B-25s started their run to the deck from 15,000 ft and literally ran off and left us behind.

'We were right behind them as they were bombing and strafing the harbour, and by the time we overflew the harbour the AAA was in full operation. It was quite a spectacular sight to see the coordinated attack as we were jinking through the flak. We finally caught up with the B-25s again at about 10,000 ft. We were supposed to be their escort, but in reality I was yelling, "Wait for me – I am your leader!"'

Maj Ed McComas, leading the 118th TRS, scored the only confirmed victory of the mission when he shot down a Ki-44 'Tojo' just north of Hong Kong island. This was the first of 14 aerial successes that he would claim between 16 October and 24 December 1944.

The very next day (17 October), the 76th FS scored its last two confirmed victories of the war. The squadron was attacking Tien Ho airfield, near Canton, at the time, and the kills were credited to Lts William Eldridge and Paul J Smith.

It was the 75th FS's turn to shine in November. By then the unit had a new commander in the form of Maj Clyde B Slocumb, who was yet another pilot starting his second tour in China – he had previously flown with the 16th FS during the 23rd FG's formative period in 1942-43. At

Chinese cities, such as Liuchow shown here, suffered terrible damage during the Japanese *Ichi-Go* advance of 1944-45 (*Art Goodworth*)

0700 hrs on 11 November, 16 P-51s of the 75th took off from Chihkiang for a sweep along the Hsiang River Valley. According to intelligence reports, the Japanese had moved numerous aircraft into the former Fourteenth Air Force bases over the previous few days. The squadron's four flights flew together as far as Lingling, where they split into two formations. Lt Don Lopez led eight fighters south to Kweilin, while Capt Stan Kelley took the rest north to Hengyang.

The reports were accurate, as the Japanese had been loading up the airfield at Hengyang for a week or more. Having received warning of the approaching raid, Japanese fighters were airborne, and they jumped Kelley's Mustangs from out of the clouds. Three P-51s went down almost immediately, but then the USAAF pilots began to gain the upper hand. Lopez, meanwhile, heard about the fight over his radio and turned his P-51s toward Hengyang. When they arrived on the scene a few minutes later, the outcome was assured.

Lt Mervin Beard was a member of Kelley's flight that day, and he wrote this account upon his return to Chihkiang;

'It was the first time I had ever shot at a real enemy aeroplane, and my first burst surprised me, as we were in a tight turn. My tracers looked as though they were curving to the outside of the turn – I could have sworn that the barrels of my guns were bent! It didn't take me long to figure it out. He crossed in front of me, and this time I used some lead and got a hit. But he didn't go down. Unless he blows up in front of you, it is hard to know what happened when you are spending as much time looking behind you as ahead.

'I pulled up to get some altitude, and as I looked down I saw several aeroplanes go into the ground. I couldn't tell whose they were, but they were silver in colour. I didn't have much time to think about it, as there were three Japs coming in on my tail, so I dove for the deck. I saw 500 mph on my airspeed indicator, and it was almost impossible to move the stick, but I finally got the aeroplane going back up. It was a close one – the trees were getting pretty big.

'I had outrun them, but they were still coming, so I turned into a bank of nearby clouds. As soon as I was sure they hadn't followed me into the clouds, I turned to 330 degrees and headed for home. I was alone, and I began to wonder what had happened to everybody. I soon had other things to think about, as my propeller was in high rpm, commonly known as "running away". I had no control of the pitch, so I slowed the aeroplane down to where I could just maintain my altitude, and prayed I would make it back.

'I soon found a checkpoint I recognised, and made the necessary correction to head into the field. When I attempted to put the wheels down I found I had no hydraulics, so I had to pump the wheels down by hand. I guess I landed with a teacup full of gas.'

Lt Beard had been lucky, but luck had not been with the three P-51 pilots who went down. Lt Robert P Miller was killed and Lt James Taylor taken prisoner. Lt Jack Gadberry baled out safely and eventually rejoined the squadron. On the plus side, the 75th FS was credited with eight confirmed victories in the fight, and two pilots – Lt Lopez and Capt Forrest 'Pappy' Parham – had scored their fifth kills to become the squadron's last two aces.

When the pilots got back to Chihkiang and Maj Slocumb heard about the fight, he immediately put together another Hengyang mission to try to catch the enemy aircraft on the ground. Lt Lopez was assigned to lead the operation, since he was familiar with the territory, and Slocumb tagged along in a wingman slot. The Mustang pilots found just a few Ki-43s parked at Hengyang, and Slocumb was credited with destroying one of them. But the 75th FS had done the job.

After the war, the Japanese admitting pulling back their fighters to Paliuchi, near Tungting Lake, after the 11 November action because the Hengyang field was too vulnerable to air attack from Chihkiang.

GUERILLA OPERATIONS

With the loss of Liuchow in mid-November, two squadrons needed new bases. The 76th FS was sent to Luliang, where bad weather severely limited the squadron's operations for the remainder of the year. The 118th TRS got a better deal. Maj McComas led his Mustangs to Suichuan, in the Chinese-held pocket between Hankow and Canton, where they would be able to carry out guerilla operations just as the 74th FS was doing at Kanchow. As these two squadrons reached ever further into Japanese-held territory during December and January, their pilots would have the opportunity to run up impressive scores of enemy aircraft destroyed both in the air and on the ground.

Maj 'Pappy' Herbst of the 74th FS made special plans for a mission on 8 December. Hoping to remind the Japanese of their turn of fortune since

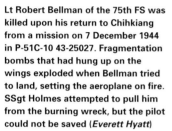

Lt Robert Bellman of the 75th FS was killed upon his return to Chihkiang from a mission on 7 December 1944 in P-51C-10 43-25027. Fragmentation bombs that had hung up on the wings exploded when Bellman tried to land, setting the aeroplane on fire. SSgt Holmes attempted to pull him from the burning wreck, but the pilot could not be saved (*Everett Hyatt*)

the Pearl Harbor raid three years earlier, he chose the former capital of China, Nanking (Nanjing), as the target for his squadron's next long-range strike. The city was farther east on the Yangtze River than the Mustangs had ventured before. More importantly, it had substantial shipping facilities, and its two airfields were believed to be packed with Japanese aircraft.

Herbst assigned Lt Ken LaTourelle to lead the mission. His 16 P-51s flew from Kanchow to the remote field at Nancheng on the morning of 8 December to refuel, and then proceeded north to Wuhu as a diversion before turning northeast and following the river into Nanking. Eight of the Mustangs were carrying bombs, and these aircraft attacked a railway ferry on the river, as well as nearby dock facilities. Four Ki-43s circled out from behind a mountain as the seventh P-51 began its bombing run. By this time, the leading Mustangs had completed their attacks and were zooming back up to altitude, so they were able to engage the oncoming 'Oscars' without calling in the top cover flight. Capt Robert E Brown scored one confirmed destroyed and one probable in this quick scrap.

The formation then proceeded to Ming Ku Kung and Tai Chao Chan airfields and found aeroplanes parked all over them. The top cover came down to join the strafing, and the pilots set up irregular attack patterns over both bases so as to throw off the aim of the anti-aircraft defences. In just a few minutes the marauding Mustang pilots destroyed no fewer than 18 enemy aircraft on the two airfields. Lt LaTourelle took top honors with three destroyed and two damaged in four passes. In all, at least 11 pilots destroyed at least one aircraft.

Lts Fred L Richardson (left) and Russell F 'Rusty' Packard (right) pose with Sgt Moyle, the crew chief of the 118th TRS P-51C-11 ('591' 44-11105 *Martha*) that they shared. Packard recalled, 'Moyle was one hell of a mechanic, and I was never kept on the ground because of mechanical trouble' (*'Rusty' Packard*)

Meanwhile, several Japanese fighters attempted to attack the strafers, but they soon found themselves under fire – two were downed by Lt John W Bolyard. His first victim was identified as a Ki-61 'Tony', which was a type rarely seen in China. Bolyard attacked his opponent from head-on at 4000 ft, but the 'Tony' scissored underneath. The Japanese pilot repeated this manoeuvre several times before finally being hit and crashing north of Tai Chao Chan.

Bolyard climbed up over the airfield and next spotted a Ki-84 'Frank' flying south. The performance of the latter fighter was considered roughly equal to that of the Mustang, but that did not come into play in this case because the Japanese pilot apparently was not paying attention to his tail. Bolyard closed in right behind his victim and opened fire at close range. The 'Frank' burst into flames and spun into the ground.

Bolyard would become an ace several weeks later when he shot down a Ki-44 over Canton for his fifth, and last, victory.

Additional single aerial successes were confirmed for Lts Heston 'Tony' Cole and Wallace Cousins, and only one P-51 was lost. Lt Frederick McGill's aeroplane was hit in the propeller by ground fire whilst strafing the ferry, and he nursed the aeroplane until it was 20 miles away from Nanking, whereupon he took to his parachute.

Daily operations continued, but the next big excitement came on 18 December when Brig Gen Chennault arranged an all-out attack against Hankow that was designed to hamper, if not cripple, the Japanese offensive by knocking out this key supply centre. This long-sought after mission would involve not only fighters and bombers of nearly all Fourteenth Air Force units, but also Twentieth Air Force B-29s based at Chengtu that heretofore had been bombing Manchuria and Japan with limited success.

Three of the 23rd FG squadrons took part. The 75th FS escorted B-24s of the 308th BG that were assigned to attack an airfield. The bombers made clean runs over the target and plastered Hankow without encountering any enemy opposition – all the P-51s involved returned to Chihkiang.

It was a different story for the two 'guerrilla' squadrons. The 74th FS sent off 18 P-51s to escort B-25s to Wuchang, with Maj Phil Chapman leading and the new group commander, Col Ed Rector, at the head of Red Flight. The B-25s attacked a satellite airfield 30 minutes after the B-29s had struck the city, their bomb run being timed to catch Japanese fighters refuelling after the Superfortress attack. Things did not go to plan, however, as the Mustang pilots engaged a flight of 'Oscars' directly overhead the field and claimed five destroyed. Although the 74th FS had enjoyed success, there were few targets on the ground for the B-25s' bombs. As the Mitchells headed for home, the P-51s turned east to sweep the Yangtze River as far as Kiukiang.

The 74th FS pilots found a gold mine of parked aircraft on the airfield at Kiukiang (Jiujiang), burning ten and damaging several more – Capt Floyd Finberg was credited with six destroyed. Fellow Mustang pilot Lt John Wheeler was hit by ground fire and had to bale out deep inside enemy territory southeast of Hankow. Fortunately, he was found by a group of US guerrillas who were operating an underground Chinese army. They helped him arrange transport back to his base at Kanchow.

Very clean P-51B '118' displays the 'Pontiac' Indian-head tail marking adopted by the 76th FS. Most of the squadron's Mustangs also carried the black-banded propeller spinner seen here on this aircraft (*Art Flatt*)

The 118th TRS had a familiar guest along on its 18 December mission – Lt Col Charles Older, deputy commander of the 23rd FG. Older was a former AVG ace who had returned to China in the summer of 1944, and had since flown quite a few missions with the 118th.

On the 18th, recently promoted Lt Col Ed McComas led 17 Mustangs from Suichuan on a similar mission to the 74th's, escorting B-25s attacking the main airfield at Wuchang. This time the timing strategy worked, and the Mitchells bombed an airfield packed with targets. The 118th then escorted them a safe distance toward home, before turning back to strafe the enemy airfield.

Four Ki-43s were spotted in the air as the 118th arrived to begin its strafing runs. Lt Col Older caught up with one of them and hit it with a telling burst in the cockpit and wing root area. Older then overshot the target, but his wingman, Lt Everson Pearsall, saw the 'Oscar' crash off the end of the airfield. A second confirmed kill was credited to Lt Carlton Covey of the 118th.

With the sky now cleared of enemy interceptors, the 118th was free to thoroughly strafe the airfield. Seven more aeroplanes were destroyed on the ground in the face of light ground fire, and all the P-51s returned safely to Suichuan. Lt Col Older would down three more aircraft the following day when he returned to Wuchang on a solo reconnaissance mission.

The 23rd FG had not played a central role in the 18 December assault on Hankow. The bulk of the destruction had been caused by the B-29s and their incendiary bombs, which started fires that burned out large sections of the city. But the group did receive credit for destroying 24 enemy aircraft, which was a good day's work on any war front.

Lt Col Charles H Older rests on a bomb at Laohwangping with a 118th TRS Mustang parked behind him. Older scored ten victories with the AVG and then added eight more during a second tour in China as deputy commander of the 23rd FG. This tally saw him tie with Lt Col John C 'Pappy' Herbst for the position of top ace in the CBI. Older became a judge after the war (*Ray Crowell*)

At this time, an 'ace race' was heating up in the 23rd FG. Maj 'Pappy' Herbst scored his 11th victory on 18 December after a two-month drought. Lt Col McComas scored his fifth and sixth victories on 19 December to become his squadron's second ace, and he added two more kills over Hong Kong on 21 December. Since returning to China, Lt Col Older had added five victories to the ten he scored with the AVG in 1941-42.

Two days before Christmas, Lt Col McComas took a big jump toward the scoring lead when the 118th TRS sent 16 Mustangs to attack the Hankow-Wuchang ferry docks on the Yangtze River. The flight was intercepted by a strong force of Ki-43s, and the Mustang pilots claimed eight victories for the loss of one of their own. But what made the fight extraordinary was that five of the kills fell to McComas alone. It was the highest total ever credited to one pilot for a single mission in the history of the 23rd FG. The following combat report described McComas' feat;

'McComas, leading the cover flight, made several passes on the Wuchang airfield, probably destroying one "Lily" and damaging an "Oscar" on the ground. As he pulled up off these passes, he observed six "Oscars" above him. One "Oscar" tailed him and scored hits on his wing, but McComas dived away and then climbed to 7000 ft and tailed one "Oscar" from astern. He fired a long burst at this "Oscar" and saw hits

Lt Col Ed McComas, seen here in his well-known Mustang '600', became a contender for top ace of the 23rd FG by scoring 14 confirmed victories in the last three months of 1944 while commanding the 118th TRS. The extra flags on the scoreboard may indicate ground kills (*Ray Crowell*)

going into the wing root. The Jap pilot jettisoned his canopy and baled out. One confirmed on this.

'Two more "Oscars" jumped McComas, who headed southeast toward Kiukiang. He passed over Erh Tao Kao and saw nine "Oscars" preparing to take off. He circled and made a west-to-east pass on two more "Oscars" just as they cleared the runway on take-off. He fired a good burst into one "Oscar", which flipped over and crashed into the other, and both crashed just east of the field. Two confirmed on this.

'McComas then motored up behind two other "Oscars" after they took off abreast. McComas closed to within 50 ft of them and fired a long burst into each. He observed them both to crash east of the field. Two confirmed on this.'

McComas scored once more the following day to bring his score to 14, – one ahead of Herbst and just one behind Older. McComas scored no further kills, however, as his combat tour was coming to an end. Herbst claimed two more victories on 27 December during a sweep of airfields at Canton to tie Older with 15 kills apiece, and there the 'ace race' would stand as the 23rd FG entered the new year, 1945.

The weather socked in on New Year's Day in eastern China, which was bad news for the guerilla squadrons at Kanchow and Suichuan. The Japanese took the opportunity to launch a ground advance aimed at taking these pesky bases while the aircraft there were grounded. The Japanese drew closer and closer, but neither the 74th FS nor the 118th TRS could turn a propeller until 13 January. By then it was clear that both

Above
Capt Oran S Watts, centre, who assumed command of the 118th TRS in January 1945, and was its first ace, poses with his squadron leadership team at Sichuan. They are, from left to right, Frank Palmer (B Flight), Ray Crowell (A Flight), Melvin Scheer (assistant operations officer), Watts, Carl Colleps (D Flight), Blanton Keller (operations officer) and Maurice Wells (C Flight) (*Ray Crowell*)

Left
Col Ed Rector (left) pins a medal on Lt Col John C 'Pappy' Herbst, whose 18 confirmed victories tied him with Chuck Older for top ace in the 23rd FG. Herbst, who had flown in the RCAF early in the war, was killed when his P-80A crashed during an airshow in San Diego, California, on 4 July 1946 (*Leon Klesman*)

bases would have to be abandoned sooner or later, but Col Ed Rector was determined to get in a few last licks at the enemy before then. He sent the 74th FS to hit Anking on 14 December, and the 118th TRS attacked Hong Kong and Canton the following day. But the veteran Rector had saved the best for last.

On 16 January, 'Pappy' Herbst shot down two enemy aircraft north of Formosa to take the scoring lead. That same day, a photo-reconnaissance aeroplane brought back pictures showing a big build-up of enemy aircraft at the five airfields in and around Shanghai. Intelligence officers speculated that the Japanese had moved the aeroplanes to the great port city at the mouth of the Yangtze to save them from being destroyed or captured in the Philippines.

Shanghai would be the farthest objective ever hit by the guerilla squadrons, but it was well within the range of their Mustangs. Rector gathered 20 P-51s from both squadrons and sent them to refuel at Nancheng on the morning of 17 January. They took off from there at 1050 hrs for the 2½-hour flight to Shanghai, with Lt Col Older leading eight aircraft of the 118th TRS and Maj Phil Chapman heading the assault flights of the 74th. Maj 'Pappy' Herbst tagged along with 'observer' status as part of the latter squadron's top cover.

The formation circled past Shanghai and attacked from the east. Achieving complete surprise, Older's flight dived on Tachang airfield from 10,000 ft. Older was at 2000 ft on his first pass when he saw a Ki-51 'Sonia' flying in front of him. He gave the observation aeroplane a quick burst, and it crashed east of the field. He completed his strafing pass, then saw two more Japanese aircraft flying low near the river. Quickly catching them up, Older fired at each one from behind and watched them both fall

A technician works in the cockpit of Lt Col Chuck Older's P-51D '129' 44-11276 *YOKAHAMA YARDBIRD*. It was named for a relative of Older who was being held as a prisoner of war in Japan (*Art Flatt*)

'Pappy' Herbst's P-51B '40' of
the 74th FS taxis at Kanchow
in January 1945. The aeroplane
displays one swastika in addition
to the Japanese flags on Herbst's
scoreboard, but no documentation
for this victory, which he claimed
to have scored in Europe with the
RCAF, has ever surfaced
(*Bernard Fudge*)

away to crash into the river. He then made several more strafing runs over
the field, noting very light ground fire, and succeeded in setting at least
three more aeroplanes on fire.

Aside from these aerial successes, the total number of ground kills
credited to the unit at Tachang was 11, and all of the 118th's aircraft
returned safely. The 74th FS struck Lungwha and Hungjao airfields with
even greater success, tallying no fewer than 57 aircraft destroyed on the
ground – Maj Chapman and Lt Wade Terry of the 74th were credited
with ten ground victories apiece. The 74th pilots (led by Lt Ira Binkley)
who attacked Hungjao accounted for another 30 aeroplanes destroyed on
the ground.

'Pappy' Herbst also enjoyed success, shooting down one of two Ki-44s
that he spotted flying together. His victory, and the three scored by Older,
left them tied as the leading aces in China with 18 victories apiece. Neither
pilot would score again, nor would anyone else even approach their totals
during the remaining months of the war in the CBI.

The grand total for the 17 January mission was 73 Japanese aircraft
destroyed on the ground and in the air, making it the most destructive
single mission ever flown by the 23rd FG.

Three days later, as preparations were being made to abandon the
guerilla bases, the 23rd FG struck Shanghai once again. This time, the
118th would revisit the three airfields attacked previously, while the
74th hit Woosung and Kiangwan, which had not been targeted on 17
January. This time, however, poor visibility due to a heavy layer of smoke
over Shanghai severely hampered the operation, and the results were
less impressive.

During their run in to Lungwha (the 118th's primary target), the
Mustang pilots, led by Lt Russ Williams, spotted several Japanese fighters
flying in their vicinity. Williams peeled off to make a pass at an Imperial
Japanese Naval Air Force A6M Zero-sen fighter that was in the landing
pattern. He hit the aircraft and it exploded, but as Williams flew past his

113

Lt Russell D Williams of the 118th TRS became the last ace of the 23rd FG when he scored his fifth victory on 20 January 1945 over Shanghai. Note that the personal markings on this P-51 have been taped onto the fighter expressly for this publicity photograph (*Ray Crowell*)

Lt Alfred Griffy of the 74th FS was assigned to fly *Rose's Raider* after its previous pilot, Lt Ed Beethoven, completed his combat tour. Like many Mustangs of the 74th FS in 1945, this P-51B has an all-black nose and carries a scoreboard denoting its pilot's combined air and ground victories – in this case six flags (*Al Griffy*)

victim the Mustang's left wing clipped the burning aeroplane, causing major damage to the P-51. Nevertheless, the Zero-sen represented Williams' fifth victory, thus making him the very last pilot to achieve ace status whilst serving with the 23rd FG. He managed to nurse his damaged Mustang (camouflaged P-51B '597') back to Suichuan and perform a safe landing.

Now, with another spell of bad weather closing in, Rector made the sad decision to pull his squadrons out of Suichuan and Kanchow. The 118th TRS flew to Luliang on 22 January, and the 74th FS followed the next day. A skeleton crew with four Mustangs remained at Kanchow until

4 February, when Maj Phil Chapman finally ordered the base destroyed prior to leading his flight to Luliang, some four hours flying time away.

THE HOME STRETCH

Air-to-air encounters with the enemy became increasingly rare after January, for the Japanese had pulled what few aircraft remained in fighting condition back to the Shanghai-Nanking area to provide air defence for these key cities. That did not mean the action was over for the 23rd FG, however, as ground attack missions of all kinds continued throughout the final six months of the war.

The 75th FS remained at Chihkiang through the spring of 1945. The 76th FS moved up to a new base at Laohwangping, not far from Chihkiang, but remained grounded by bad weather until spring. At Luliang, the 74th FS and 118th TRS were too far from the front to reach any meaningful targets.

With the arrival of better weather in the spring, the 74th FS moved to a new base at Tushan, about 300 miles east of Luliang. From there, the Mustangs were within range of potential targets in the Hsiang River Valley and at Canton and Hong Kong. The 118th TRS joined the 76th FS at Laohwangping after a stay at Chengkung.

Although the Mustang pilots now had little reason to worry about getting shot down by enemy fighters, ground fire still posed a serious hazard. The P-51's performance was well suited to low-level work, as the aeroplane was plenty fast, manoeuvrable and capable of carrying a wide

Capt Ed Paine (left), intelligence officer of the 76th FS, briefs Lt Col Louis V Teeter and Maj David Whiddon prior to a mission in the spring of 1945. Whiddon assumed command of the 76th after Teeter was killed in action strafing Liuchow on 3 June 1945 (*Burt Greenburg*)

When the Fourteenth Air Force's numbering system changed in the spring of 1945, the 118th TRS shifted to '150-199'. Here, battered P-51C '188' gets a lift after a rough landing at Laohwangping. Note that the fighter's lightning flash does not extend behind the national insignia (*Ray Crowell*)

range of weapons. Its Achilles heel – the vulnerability of its radiator to ground fire – remained, but pilots accepted that as a fair trade-off for the Mustang's high performance.

The 74th FS got a painful reminder of the dangers of combat flying on 28 March when its new commanding officer, Maj Philip G Chapman, led a raid against Kai Tak airfield at Hong Kong. Chapman, a seven-victory ace, noted little return fire on his first pass over the field and decided to go back for another shot. This time intense AAA bracketed Chapman and his flight. Two P-51s went down, and Chapman's was badly hit. He nursed the aeroplane to Changting (a remote field in a Chinese-held pocket of

After a close call baling out of a P-51B with a faulty canopy release, Col Ed Rector chose one of the first P-51Ds to arrive in China as his personal aircraft. The 23rd FG commander had the aeroplane decorated with the group badge and red/white/blue bands signifying the three original squadrons in the group (*Russell Packard*)

territory east of Kanchow), but the damaged left wing of the Mustang stalled during the landing. The P-51 whipped into a spin and crashed to the ground, killing Chapman instantly.

Col Ed Rector also had his eye on Changting, and in late March he sent a P-51 task force drawn from the 75th and 76th FSs there to see if the base could support a resumption of guerilla operations. Rector led the first big mission from Changting – a strike against Hangchow, south of Shanghai – on 30 March with disappointing results. Then, on 2 April, Rector was at the head of a 32-aeroplane strike against the Shanghai airfields. Although a number of Mustangs were lost on the mission, no pilots were killed. On

Five of the 75th FS pilots heavily engaged in the defence of Chihkiang were, from left to right, Ed Bollen, Bob Smith, Gordon Willis, Tom McDonough and Don King. Bollen scored the 23rd FG's last aerial victory of the war on 2 April 1945 when he shot down a Ki-44 'Tojo' over Lungwha airfield, Shanghai (*Morton Sher*)

Capt John D 'Rosie' Rosenbaum of the 75th FS flew P-51D '71' *Miss Kitty III* during the final months of the war. He completed more than 75 missions before ending his combat tour in August 1945 (*Art Goodworth*)

With its new individual aircraft
identification number '72' on the
nose, P-51D *NOK OUT* of the 75th FS
undertakes a training mission from
Tsingchen in June 1945
(*Art Goodworth*)

Sgt Ruthermal (left) supervises as
75th FS armourers load five-inch
aerial rockets on a P-51D at Liuchow
in August 1945 (*Everett Hyatt*)

the plus side, Col Rector and Lt Ed Bollen of the 75th FS were credited
with confirmed aerial victories – the last two of the war for the 23rd FG.
Changting proved impractical to keep operational, and the P-51s soon
pulled back to their permanent bases.

Back at Chihkiang, the 75th FS was involved in heavy fighter-bomber
operations in April and May as its pilots supported Chinese troops
defending the base against the advancing Japanese. The enemy ultimately
failed to take the base, marking the Battle of Chihkiang as the high-water
mark of the *Ichi-Go* campaign. Soon the Japanese began to withdraw,
realising that they were unable to hold the territory that they had fought
so hard to capture. All four squadrons of the 23rd FG continued to harass
the retreating enemy for the rest of
the summer until the Japanese surrendered in August.

Three months of drudgery followed VJ-Day as the 23rd FG and
other units in China closed up shop
and turned over their aircraft to the
CAF to use in the civil war against
the Communists that everyone knew
was coming.

Finally, on 11 December 1945,
the men of the 23rd FG set sail
from Shanghai aboard the USS
Alderamin, bound for home. They
arrived in the harbour at Tacoma,
Washington, on 3 January 1946,
and the unit was deactivated. The
23rd FG's long war was over.

Maj Marvin Lubner, who was a six-victory ace with the 76th FS in 1942-43, returned to China in June 1945 to command the 118th TRS. His P-51K *Barfly* (44-11773) carried the number '199'. Lubner claimed to have flown the 23rd FG's last combat mission – a photo-reconnaissance sortie of Hong Kong harbour – on 7 September 1945, five days after the Japanese surrender (*Marv Lubner*)

POSTSCRIPT

The 23rd FG was reactivated as a unit of the Fifth Air Force on Guam on 10 October 1946, and it became a fighter wing two years later. The wing moved to the Panama Canal Zone in 1949 and then to Presque Isle Air Force Base, Maine, where it was deactivated again in 1952. The 23d Tactical Fighter Wing (TFW) was reactivated at McConnell AFB, Kansas, in 1964, and went back into combat in Vietnam the following year, flying F-105 Thunderchiefs. The 23rd TFW flew A-7Ds for much of the 1970s, before receiving its first A-10 Thunderbolts in 1980.

Flying A-10As, the 23rd logged more than 2700 combat sorties and lost only two aircraft in combat during Operations *Desert Shield* and *Desert Storm* in 1990-91. In 2002, the 23rd FW became the first fixed-wing aircraft unit stationed inside Afghanistan – its personnel operated simultaneously in support of Operations *Enduring Freedom* and *Southern Watch* for nearly six months. During this time, the 23rd flew 2148 combat missions over Afghanistan and Iraq.

At this writing, the 23rd FW is stationed at Moody AFB, Georgia, where its A-10s still proudly wear the sharksmouth marking that adorned its P-40s and P-51s in China during World War 2.

APPENDICES

APPENDIX 1

23rd FIGHTER GROUP WARTIME COMMANDING OFFICERS

Group Commander	start date
Robert Neale (civilian)	July 1942
Col Robert L Scott	July 1942
Lt Col Bruce K Holloway	January 1943
Lt Col Norval C Bonawitz	September 1943
Col David L Hill	November 1943
Lt Col Philip C Loofbourrow	October 1944
Col Edward F Rector	December 1944
Lt Col Clyde B Slocumb	December 1945 until decommissioning

Squadron Commander	start date
74th FS	
Maj Frank Schiel Jr	July 1942 (KIFA 5 December 1942)
Maj Albert J Baumler	December 1942
Maj John D Lombard	February 1943 (KIFA 30 June 1943)
Maj Norval C Bonawitz	July 1943
Capt William R Crooks	September 1943
Capt Paul N Bell	October 1943
Capt G Eugene Lundy	December 1943
Maj Arthur W Cruikshank Jr	May 1944
Capt John C Herbst	June 1944
Maj Philip G Chapman	February 1945 (KIA 28 March 1945)
Capt Floyd Finberg	March 1945
Maj Bruce C Downs	June 1945 until war's end
75th FS	
Maj David L Hill	July 1942
Maj John R Alison	December 1942
Maj Edmund R Goss	May 1943
Maj Elmer W Richardson	October 1943
Maj Philip C Loofbourrow	March 1944
Maj Donald L Quigley	June 1944 (PoW August 1944)
Maj A T House Jr	August 1944
Maj Clyde R Slocumb	November 1944 until war's end

Squadron Commander	start date
76th FS	
Maj Edward F Rector	July 1942
Maj Bruce K Holloway	December 1942
Capt Grant M Mahony	January 1943
Capt Robert Costello	June 1943
Capt James M Williams	October 1943
Capt John S Stewart	December 1943
Maj Charles E Griffith	May 1944 (KIFA 18 December 1944)
Maj Louis V Teeter	December 1944 (KIA 3 June 1945)
Maj David T Whiddon	June 1945 until war's end
118th TRS	
Maj Edward O McComas	September 1943 (in US)
Capt Oran S Watts	January 1945
Lt Col Charles C Simpson	May 1945
Capt Marvin Lubner	June 1945 until war's end
16th FS	
1Lt Harry B Young	April 1941 (in US)
Maj George W Hazlett	September 1942
Maj Harry M Pike	January 1943
Capt Robert L Liles	July 1943 until unit transferred to 51st FG
449th FS	
Capt Sam L Palmer	July 1943
Capt Lewden M Enslen	September 1943 until unit transferred to 51st FG

APPENDIX 2

23rd FIGHTER GROUP ACES

Name	Aerial Victories	Notes
Maj John C Herbst	18	74th & 76th FS (possibly 1 kill with RCAF in ETO)
Lt Col Charles H Older	18	23rd FG (includes 10 kills with AVG)
Col David L Hill	14.75	75th FS & 23rd FG (includes 9.25 kills with AVG)
Lt Col Edward O McComas	14	118th TRS
Capt John F Hampshire Jr	13	75th FS (KIA 2/5/43)
Col Bruce K Holloway	13	76th FS & 23rd FG
Robert H Neale (civilian)	13	23rd FG (all 13 kills with AVG)
Col Robert L Scott Jr	10	23rd FG
Capt John S Stewart	9	76th FS
Maj Arthur W Cruikshank Jr	8	74th FS
Maj Elmer W Richardson	8	75th FS
Col Edward F Rector	7.75	76th FS & 23rd FG (includes 3.75 kills with AVG)
Maj Philip G Chapman	7	74th FS (KIA 28/3/45)
Capt James W Little	7	75th FS (also had 1 kill in Korean War)
Maj John D Lombard	7	16th & 74th FSs (KIFA 30/6/43)
Lt Col John R Alison	6	16th & 75th FSs
Maj John G Bright	6	75th FS (includes 3 kills with AVG)
1Lt Charles A DuBois	6	76th FS
Maj Edmund R Goss	6	16th & 75th FSs
Capt Marvin Lubner	6	76th FS & 118th TRSs
Col Clinton D Vincent	6	23rd FG
Capt James M Williams	6	118th TRS
1Lt John W Bolyard	5	74th FS
1Lt Stephen J Bonner Jr	5	76th FS
Maj John G Bright	5	75th FS (includes 3 kills with AVG and 1 in MTO)
Capt Dallas A Clinger	5	16th & 74th FSs
Capt Mathew M Gordon Jr	5	75th FS
Capt William Grosvenor Jr	5	75th FS
Capt Lynn F Jones	5	74th FS
Maj Robert L Liles	5	16th FS (includes 1 kill with 51st FG)
1Lt Donald S Lopez	5	75th FS
Capt Forrest F Parham	5	75th FS
Capt Roger C Pryor	5	75th FS
Maj Donald L Quigley	5	75th FS (PoW 10/8/44)
Capt Oran S Watts	5	118th TRS
1Lt Russell D Williams	5	118th TRS
Maj Albert J Baumler	4.5	74th & 75th FS (also had 4.5 kills in Spanish Civil War)
Capt Joseph H Griffin	3	75th FS (also had 4 kills with Ninth AF)
Maj Witold A Urbanowicz	2	75th FS (also had 17 kills with RAF)
Lt Col Grant Mahony	1	76th FS (also had 4 kills with Fifth Air Force and 1 kill with 1st ACG, KIA 3/1/45)
Capt Tsang Hsi-Lan (CAF)	1	75th FS (also had 5 kills with CACW)

Note

Some sources also list Capt Melvin B Kimball, Capt Wiltz P Segura and Maj Clyde B Slocumb Jr as aces

COLOUR PLATES

1

P-40E '106' of John E Petach Jr, attached to the 75th FS, Hengyang, China, July 1942

When the 23rd FG was formed, the ex-AVG P-40Es were assigned to the 75th FS at Hengyang and the 76th FS at Kweilin. The pilots in these squadrons were a combination of newly arrived USAAF officers and a contingent of battle-tested AVG veterans who agreed to stay on long enough to help the 23rd FG get on its feet. Ex-AVG pilot Petach, flying with the 75th FS, claimed one Ki-27 destroyed, plus a probable on 6 July 1942, but died four days later when he was shot down by ground fire while dive-bombing the town of Linchuan. It is not known if Petach was flying '106', which carries the blue fuselage band of the 2nd PS/AVG, on his final mission.

2

P-40E '104' of Majs Edward F Rector and Bruce K Holloway, 76th FS, Kweilin, China, summer 1942

Since recent findings suggest all of the AVG's P-40Es were finished in Olive Drab over Neutral Grey, the two-colour topside camouflage on '104' possibly indicates that it was one of the few replacement E-models that trickled into China for the 23rd FG before improved P-40Ks began to arrive in the autumn of 1942. This aeroplane was flown by two successive commanders of the 76th FS in Majs Ed Rector and Bruce Holloway in the latter half of 1942. The latter pilot once suggested to the author that '104' may have been repainted during its service with the 76th FS.

3

P-40B '46' of Lt Thomas R Smith, 74th FS, Kunming, China, September 1942

Smith, in the first contingent of USAAF pilots assigned to the 74th FS, recorded the squadron's first confirmed victory in this ex-AVG Tomahawk when he intercepted a twin-engined Japanese reconnaissance aeroplane over Kunming on 8 September 1942. Most of the 23rd FG's P-40Bs, as the USAAF designated the aircraft, were concentrated in the 74th FS, which served as a training unit while providing air defence for Kunming through to the end of 1942. The surviving P-40Bs were transferred to Karachi, then in India, in the spring of 1943 to be used as trainers.

4

P-40E-1 '22' of Maj Harry M Pike, 16th FS, Kweilin, China, October 1942

The P-40s of the 16th FS, which was attached to the 23rd FG from the 51st FG until the autumn of 1943, were immediately distinguishable from those of the other squadrons because they displayed USAAF stars on their fuselages. Most of the Warhawks, including '22', also had a 16th FS 'Flying Wall of China' emblem applied to their fuselages. Pike, who was credited with shooting down a Japanese bomber over Kweilin on 23 November 1942, served as commanding officer of the 16th FS from January through to July 1943, when he was replaced by Capt Robert Liles. Pike in turn

transferred to 23rd FG headquarters. He was subsequently shot down on 15 September 1943 and spent the rest of the war as a PoW.

5

P-43A '149' of the 76th FS, Kunming, China, late 1942

The 23rd FG was the only group in the USAAF to register any aerial combat claims in the P-43. A handful of these Republic Lancer fighters were acquired on loan from the Chinese Air Force and used primarily for reconnaissance work because of their high-altitude capability. Capt Jeffery Wellborn of the 76th FS was returning from a reconnaissance mission over Burma in a P-43 on 2 January 1943 when he encountered a twin-engined Japanese aircraft (almost certainly a Ki-46 'Dinah') and shot it down for the only confirmed Lancer victory of the war. The few photos of 23rd FG P-43s suggest that the aeroplanes retained their CAF roundels on the undersides of both wings, but with the uppersurfaces of their wings unmarked.

6

P-40K '7' of Col Robert L Scott, 23rd FG, Kunming, China, December 1942

This P-40K was the replacement aircraft for Col Scott's original P-40E, which he called 'Old Exterminator' in his books. He flew this aeroplane in November-December 1942, just prior to returning to the US. Although '7's' scoreboard shows 12 victory flags, official records only exist for ten of Scott's victories. Col Casey Vincent, operations officer of the China Air Task Force, was the next pilot to fly this aeroplane with the 23rd FG, and he named it *Peggy* for his wife.

7

P-40K '23' of Lt Robert A O'Neill, 16th FS/23rd FG, Chanyi, China, February 1943

When the 16th FS re-equipped with new P-40Ks in early 1943, Lt O'Neill received '23'. The squadron's markings continued much as they had been on the P-40Es, including the application of a white star on blue shield on the main landing gear hubcaps. Some of these E-model Warhawks would remain in the frontline flying combat operations in China for more than a year, before finally being replaced by P-51s. O'Neill scored single victories over Japanese fighters on 27 November 1942, 28 December 1942 and 16 January 1943.

8

P-40K '110' of Capt Jeffrey O Wellborn, 76th FS, Kunming, China, spring 1943

By the spring of 1943, the 76th FS had standardised its unit markings, settling on a blue fuselage band as its squadron designator. The tail numbers applied to 76th FS aircraft at this time ranged from '100' to '149'. Jeffrey Wellborn joined the squadron in mid-September 1942, and he was forced down near enemy lines just two weeks later – he managed to make his way safely back to base. The single victory flag beneath the windscreen of this aircraft denotes Wellborn's unique P-43 Lancer victory of 2 January 1943.

9
P-40K '161' of Capt John F Hampshire, 75th FS, Kweilin, China, spring 1943

Hampshire's '161' displayed the standard 75th FS markings of this period, namely a white fuselage band and a tail number between '150' and '199', along with a red/white/blue pinwheel design on the hubcaps of its main landing gear. Noted for his aggressiveness, Hampshire became the first USAAF ace of the 75th FS when he shot down his third, fourth and fifth enemy aircraft on 27 November 1942. At the time of his death in action on 2 May 1943, he was the top-scoring active ace in China with 13 confirmed victories to his name.

10
P-40K '111' of Maj Grant Mahony, 76th FS, Lingling, China, May 1943

A veteran of the fighting in the Philippines and Java during early 1942, Mahony arrived in China in late 1942 and assumed command of the 76th FS in January 1943. He led the squadron until mid-year, scoring his fifth confirmed aerial victory in the process. Mahony returned to the CBI in 1944 with the 1st Air Commando Group before being transferred to the Pacific theatre, where he was killed in action flying a P-38 with the 8th FG on 3 January 1945. The bold application of the twin command stripes on the vertical tail of '111' is the only known use of this marking in the 23rd FG.

11
P-40K '115' of Lt Marvin Lubner, 76th FS, Hengyang, China, August 1943

Lubner borrowed the nickname of his favourite baseball team, the Brooklyn (now Los Angeles) Dodgers, for this P-40K. '115' is shown here as it looked when Lubner scored his fifth victory whilst flying it on 26 August 1943. Lubner was credited six confirmed kills (all Japanese fighters) while flying with the 76th FS between November 1942 and September 1943. He returned to China in 1945 but got no opportunity to add to his score.

12
P-40K '24' of Lt William B Hawkins, 74th FS, Kweilin, China, late summer 1943

Bill Hawkins delivered this P-40K to the 74th FS at Kunming when he first arrived in China in the autumn of 1942. It was one of the rare occasions when a green pilot was assigned a new aircraft he had flown in from India, as Hawkins got to keep '24' throughout his tour in China. The victory markings beneath the fighter's windscreen include the silhouette of a tanker, signifying the vessel Hawkins skip-bombed in Hong Kong harbour on 2 September 1943. The application of the serial number (42-46252) in black on the tail was rarely seen on 23rd FG P-40Ks of this period. Note also the second set of centreline bomb/drop tank brackets below the rear fuselage and the red propeller spinner. The latter was a 74th FS marking that was introduced at about this time.

13
P-40M '179' of Lt James L Lee, 75th FS, Kunming, China, late summer 1943

P-40Ms began to arrive in China in May-June 1943, and '179' was assigned to Lt J L 'Shorty' Lee of the 75th FS.

Lee scored two confirmed victories in April 1943, and had added two more and one damaged to his score by year end. With the P-40M, Curtiss dropped the brown/green/sky grey camouflage scheme from the Warhawk line in favour of Olive Drab over Neutral Grey. Here again we see the 75th FS 'shark' badge on '179's' tail fin and the white fuselage band.

14
P-40K '14' of Capt Clyde Slocumb, 16th FS, Yunnanyi, China, summer 1943

By the summer of 1943, 'Flying Wall of China' badges were beginning to disappear from the fuselages of 16th FS Warhawks, including this one. The main landing gear hubcaps on '14' were white with a swirl pattern on them, likely in green. The one victory flag signifies Slocumb's first claim – a Japanese bomber shot down over Kweilin on 2 November 1942. After completing his combat tour with the 16th FS in 1943, Slocumb served in the US for about a year before returning to China and assuming command of the 75th FS, which he led for the remainder of the war.

15
P-38G (no number) of 2Lt Earl E Helms, 449th FS, Kweilin, China, late summer 1943

The 449th FS arrived in China in July 1943 and was attached to the 23rd FG for about three months prior to transferring to the 51st FG. Its P-38s were not initially welcomed by Brig Gen Chennault because of their high fuel consumption, but the fighters' speed, range and altitude performance soon proved useful. Lt Helms was one of the first pilots in the 449th to score in China, claiming a Zero-sen destroyed over Hong Kong on 29 July 1943. He later added two 'Tojos' destroyed and an 'Oscar' damaged to his score. During this period 449th P-38s did not carry a squadron identification number on their radiator housings, but the unit was subsequently assigned the numbers '300-349'. Note how the hot exhaust exiting from the turbocharger has obscured the serial number on the fighter's vertical tail.

16
P-40K '1' of Col Bruce Holloway, 23rd FG, Kweilin, China, September 1943

Holloway arrived in China in May 1942 with an assignment to observe AVG operations, and he flew several uneventful missions with the group before it disbanded. When the 23rd FG was formed in July 1942, Holloway became executive officer, then served as 76th FS commander for a short time, before assuming command of the group when Col Scott departed in January 1943. By the time Holloway received orders sending him back to the US in the autumn of 1943, his 13 confirmed victories ranked him as the leading active ace in the CBI. This P-40K was badly shot up while being flown by another pilot on 8 September 1943, and Holloway had left China before it was returned to operational status.

17
P-40K '36' of Lt Fred L Meyer, 74th FS, Kweilin, China, autumn 1943

Fred Meyer joined the 74th FS in mid-April 1943 at Yunnanyi as a replacement pilot, and he experienced the devastating Japanese bombing raid on the base later that month. On 9 September 1943 he was badly shot up in a scrap near Canton while flying Col Holloway's P-40, but managed to nurse the aeroplane back to base at Kweilin. Meyer did all of his scoring in December 1943, claiming one Ki-43 destroyed, one probable and three damaged in the course of two missions at Hengyang. Note the extended trim tab on the rudder of '36'. This aeroplane eventually came to grief in a belly landing at Kweilin in the spring of 1944.

18

P-40K '171' of Maj Elmer Richardson, 75th FS, Hengyang, China, late 1943

Richardson flew fighters in the Canal Zone before being sent to China in the autumn of 1942, where he used his flying experience to good effect when he entered combat. A year later, Richardson was both a six-victory ace and commanding officer of the 75th FS, as signified by the twin white stripes on the fuselage of his P-40K. In December 1943, after having transferred to 23rd FG headquarters, he scored twice more, and also added a ground victory. '171' displays the change in markings adopted by the 75th FS at this time, which included painting the forward section of the propeller spinner white and repositioning the individual aircraft number to the tail. The latter change would allow room for the star-and-bar national insignia to be applied to the fuselage, although that has not yet been done to this aircraft.

19

P-40N '21' of Capt Harlyn Vidovich, 74th FS, Kweilin, China, December 1943

Vidovich, a full-blooded Paiute-Shoshone Indian, flew his first combat mission from Kweilin with the 74th FS in May 1943. Less than a month later he submitted his first claim – an enemy fighter probably destroyed at Hengyang – and he added two confirmed victories to his tally by the end of the year. Vidovich was killed when his fighter crashed during bad weather on 18 January 1944. As one of the first P-40N-5s to arrive in China, '21' has been modified with the larger main landing gear wheels of the earlier Warhawk models. These were fitted because there was a supply of replacement tyres in China for the older wheels but not for the smaller 27-inch wheels of new model Warhawks.

20

P-51A '122' of Capt John S Stewart, 76th FS, Suichwan, China, February-March 1944

This aircraft was amongst the first Mustangs transferred from the 311th FBG in India to China in the autumn of 1943 and concentrated within the 76th FS. The P-51As saw their first action in-theatre during the Thanksgiving Day 1943 raid on Formosa. '122' displays the final score of Capt John Stewart, the leading ace and commanding officer of the 76th FS who was credited with shooting down five Japanese fighters, three bombers and one transport aeroplane between 23 July 1943 and 12 February 1944. The aircraft carried the name of Stewart's wife on its nose, as did his earlier P-40s.

21

P-40N '45' of Maj Arthur Cruikshank, 74th FS, Hengyang, China, June 1944

One of the original pilots of the 74th 'school' squadron,

Art Cruikshank learned his lessons well by becoming the first ace to score all of his victories while serving in the squadron. He completed his first combat tour in June 1943 and returned to China the following May to assume command of his old squadron. Eager to add to his score of six confirmed kills, Cruikshank claimed two more victories on 25 June 1944. He was shot down the next day, but managed to evade capture and returned to his squadron in August. Cruikshank was sent home shortly thereafter. This P-40N, which was Cruikshank's penultimate mount, displays the 74th FS badge on its rudder.

22

P-40N '22' of Capt Charles E Cook Jr, 74th FS, Kweilin, China, summer 1944

'Smokey' Cook was a replacement pilot who arrived in China in late 1943 and quickly made his mark by damaging a Ki-43 during a fight near Hengyang on 10 December. By August 1944 he was a battle-tested veteran heavily involved in the air campaign over the Hsiang Valley with a score of two confirmed victories, two probables (signified by the half-flags on his scoreboard) and one damaged. '22' has a replacement cowling that lacks a 'sharksmouth' and a red propeller spinner, which the 74th FS used during this period as a squadron marking. This aeroplane was transferred to the CACW's 5th FG at Chihkiang after the 74th FS transitioned to P-51s.

23

P-51B '11' of Col David L Hill, 23rd FG, Kweilin, China, summer 1944

The legendary 'Tex' Hill, veteran ace of the AVG and CATF, returned to China in November 1943 to assume command of the 23rd FG. He took this P-51B-2 as his personal aircraft soon after the Merlin-powered Mustangs began arriving in March 1944 – the aeroplane was carried on the records of the 74th FS. It is likely that Hill scored his last confirmed victory in '11' while leading a bomber escort mission to Hankow on 6 May 1944. That brought his total to 14.75 destroyed. Hill continued flying the aeroplane throughout the summer, before eventually returning to the US in October 1944.

24

P-51C '103' of Lt Robert Schaeffer, 76th FS, Liuchow, China, autumn 1944

Bob Schaeffer had not been in China for long when he was shot down in a P-40 on 27 December 1943 near Suichuan in the combat that is depicted on the cover of this book. Back in action three days later, again over Suichuan, he evened the score by shooting down a Japanese fighter that he identified as a 'Zero', but which was almost certainly a Ki-43. Schaeffer's second victory, over a Ki-44, came during a scrap east of Tungting Lake on 29 August 1944. *JEANNE IV* displays the standard 76th FS markings of the period – a blue propeller spinner and three-digit tail number.

25

P-51C '187' of Capt Forrest Parham, 75th FS, Chihkiang, China, November 1944

The last active ace of the 75th FS, 'Pappy' Parham did all of his scoring in roughly three months from August through to November 1944. He scored his fifth, and last, victory over Hengyang on 11 November in the same combat that saw fellow 75th FS ace Lt Don Lopez also score his fifth kill. Parham remained on operations into the spring of 1945, and was shot down on a long-range strike against the airfields at Shanghai on 2 April. He baled out and escaped from behind enemy lines, returning to his squadron a month later. The black tail and stripe on '187' was the 75th FS unit marking from late 1944 through to the end of the war.

26

F-6C '600' of Maj Edward McComas, 118th TRS, Suichwan, China, November 1944

The very aggressive Ed McComas led the 118th TRS to China in mid-1944 with the personal goal of becoming the top ace in-theatre, and he almost succeeded. Although sidelined by an illness during the squadron's first months in action, he scored 14 confirmed victories between 16 October and 24 December 1944. McComas' tally included five victories on 23 December, making him the Fourteenth Air Force's only 'ace in a day'. Although McComas' P-51D '600' is better known, the ace did most of his scoring in this F-6C. Mustangs of the 118th TRS displayed many variations on the squadron's 'black lightning' markings scheme.

27

P-51B '40' of Maj John C Herbst, 74th FS, Kanchow, China, January 1945

Starting in June 1944, 'Pappy' Herbst tallied 18 confirmed victories in seven months of combat flying in China to become the top-scoring ace of the Fourteenth Air Force. He also claimed to have scored one victory while flying with the Royal Canadian Air Force in Europe earlier in the war, which explains the single swastika in the extensive scoreboard on his '40' Mustang. Herbst named the aeroplane in honour of his young son, Tommy. Upon his return to the US, Herbst joined the 412th FG, which was the USAAF's first jet-equipped unit. He was killed when the Shooting Star that he was displaying crashed at an airshow in San Diego on 4 July 1946.

28

P-51B '48' of Lt Ira Binkley, 74th FS, Kanchow, China, January 1945

Binkley's Mustang, like Herbst's, displays the very plain markings (consisting merely of a two-digit tail number) that adorned 74th FS Mustangs during this period. The key difference is that the scoreboard on this P-51 includes the pilot's credits for 11 ground kills as well as for his single aerial victory – standard practice in the 74th FS and 118th TRS starting in late 1944. Binkley claimed six ground kills on 17 January 1945 when he led a surprise attack on Shanghai's Hungjao airfield. Promoted to captain in April 1945, Binkley subsequently returned to the US two months later.

29

P-51D (no number) of Col Edward Rector, 23rd FG, Luliang, China, spring 1945

AVG and CATF veteran Ed Rector, on his second combat tour in China, was nearly killed in late 1944 when the canopy jammed on his stricken P-51B as he was trying to take to his parachute. He eventually got free of the aeroplane, baled out successfully and evaded capture. Upon returning to the group, Rector grounded all the Mustangs in the 23rd FG until their canopies could be checked. He also snapped up one of the first bubble-canopy P-51Ds to arrive in China as his personal aircraft. The three bands around the rear fuselage mark this as a P-51 assigned to a headquarters pilot. Rector commanded the group through to the end of the war.

30

P-51D '125' of Lt Col Charles Older, 23rd FG HQ, Luliang, China, spring 1945

Chuck Older was already a double ace, with ten victories scored in the AVG, when he returned to China for a second tour in the summer of 1944 – Older served as group operations officer and deputy commander of the 23rd FG. He claimed eight more victories between 28 July 1944 and 17 January 1945 to tie with 'Pappy' Herbst as the leading American ace in the CBI. After the war, Older had a distinguished legal career, and in 1967 was appointed to the bench of the Los Angeles Superior Court. His most famous case was the Charles Manson murder trial. Note the misspelling of YOKAHAMA in name on the nose of the fighter.

31

P-51C '113' of Lt Donald L Scott, 76th FS, Laohwangping, China, spring 1945

Over the winter of 1944-45, the 76th FS adorned its P-51s with a Pontiac Indian head profile, which was chosen to match the squadron's radio call sign. The design was painted white on Don Scott's aircraft, the last camouflaged Mustang in the squadron. Named for a girl Scott was dating when he went overseas in mid-1944, the aeroplane was destroyed on 22 May 1945 after it was hit on the ground during a night bombing raid. Scott went on to complete 28 combat missions prior to returning to the US in September 1945.

32

P-51C '591' of Lts Fred L Richardson Jr and Russell E Packard, 118th TRS, Chengkung, China, spring 1945

'Rusty' Packard joined the 118th TRS in January 1945 and had completed 12 combat missions by war's end. As pilot strength built up in the 118th during 1945, it became common practice to assign two junior pilots to a single aircraft, as was the case with '591'. Each pilot took one side of the fuselage for his personal markings, thus this aircraft carried on its starboard side the name Billie and Packard's name below the cockpit, plus the sentiment Still, Who Cares with a small pin-up illustration below the exhausts. The aeroplane became '191' when the 118th's numbers changed in the spring of 1945.

33

P-51K '143' of Lt Benjamin R Thompson, 76th FS, Laohwangping, China, June 1945

Ben Thompson flew P-40s and P-51s during his tour with the 76th FS, which ran from September 1944 through to July 1945. He recalled that fellow pilot Capt Bill Lillie, an architect in civilian life, was the artist who not only designed the squadron's tail marking but who also adorned many of the P-51s with personal artwork such as Thompson's Bugs Bunny. The colours on the propeller spinner are unconfirmed – most pilots recall them as shown, but Thompson told the author they were dark insignia blue divided by a band of natural metal.

34
P-51D '21' of Capt John C Conn, 74th FS, Tushan, China, summer 1945

After graduating from flight school in November 1943, John Conn did a stint as an instructor in the fighter replacement training unit at Venice, in Florida, before transferring to China in the autumn of 1944. Action came thick and fast when he joined the 74th FS at Kanchow, and soon the flight experience he gained as an instructor began to pay off. On 17 January 1945, Conn was credited with seven ground kills during that day's mass attacks on enemy airfields in Shanghai. His tally of ground victories had grown to nine by the time he was assigned this brand new P-51D, which he duly named for his girlfriend and future wife.

35
P-51D '71' of Capt John D Rosenbaum, 75th FS, Liuchow, China, August 1945

'Rosie' Rosenbaum flew an eventful tour of more than 75 missions with the 75th FS between the summer of 1944 and August 1945. Early on, his P-40N was shot up during an air battle over Hengyang on 4 August 1944, but he managed to nurse it back to Kweilin. Rosenbaum was credited with two Japanese fighters damaged in air combats on 16 September and 11 November, and his last claim was for an enemy aircraft probably destroyed on the ground at Sintsiang on 20 December 1944. *Miss Kitty III* displays the late-war markings of the 75th FS, with its two-digit squadron number on the lower cowling.

36
P-51K '199' of Maj Marvin Lubner, 118th TRS, Laohwangping, China, August 1945

When six-victory ace Marv Lubner returned to China in June 1945, he was assigned as commanding officer of the 118th TRS. By this time, the 23rd FG had realigned the number assignments for its squadrons, with the 118th getting the '150-199' sequence. It was possibly in '199' that Lubner flew what he considered to be the 23rd FG's final mission of World War 2 – a photo-reconnaissance of Hong Kong on 7 September 1945, some five days after Japan had formally surrendered in ceremonies that took place aboard the battleship USS *Missouri* as it was anchored in Tokyo Bay. He would fly photo-reconnaissance missions again during the Korean conflict.

COLOUR SECTION

1
Mustangs of the 75th FS/23rd FG are parked on the former Japanese airfield at Hangchow in October 1945. Note the P-47 Thunderbolts parked neatly behind the P-51s (*Dwayne Tabatt*)

2
Col Ed Rector's P-51D 44-11293 is parked with 76th FS Mustangs at Shanghai in late 1945. The tail of the 76th FS's Vultee BT-13 hack can be seen to the right of the Mustang (*Bud Biteman*)

3
Lt Philip Dickey, armaments officer for the 118th TRS, poses with one of the first Mustangs in the squadron to be marked up with the 'black lightning' design. Dickey created this marking following a direct request from his CO, Lt Col Ed McComas. According to his nephew Maj Robert Bourlier, 'Lt Dickey was well liked and respected by the officers and men of the 118th, and he was well known as an artist. While in India, he was called upon by several pilots to add their names and some artwork to their P-40s. After the unit received their P-51B/Cs in China, he was again asked to paint some of the aeroplanes. During the summer of 1944, Lt Col McComas told Lt Dickey to design a distinctive squadron marking for the aeroplanes. Within a few days the "Black Lightning" marking had been produced and the first aeroplane (aircraft "599") painted up. After several flights Lt Col McComas felt that the lightning bolt did not stand out. There was some yellow paint available that was used for creating signs on base, and this was used to good effect to outline the new markings' (*via Robert Bourlier*)

4
This A-10 Thunderbolt of the 75th FS flew in Operation *Desert Storm* and performed an aerobatics display for the 23rd FG reunion at Eglin Air Force Base, Florida, in October 1991 (*Carl Molesworth*)

ACKNOWLEDGEMENTS

Hundreds of 23rd FG veterans and their families have supported my research over the past 30 years, and I deeply appreciate every one of their contributions. However, one man stands out above all of them – the late Lt Col Donald S Lopez, USAF-retired – for the unwavering cooperation and encouragement he gave from the very beginning. I first met Don when he agreed to grant an interview to me, an unknown writer, for a magazine article that I wanted to write about his experiences as an ace in the 75th Fighter Squadron. From that day in 1978 until his death in 2008, Don provided me not only with material about the 23rd FG, but also the encouragement to keep digging for more. Thanks to him, I was able to gain access to all of those other great men who served in the group in China between 1942-45. In appreciation, I dedicate this book to Don Lopez, for without him, it could not have happened.

BIBLIOGRAPHY

BARNUM, BURRALL, *Dear Dad*. Richard R Smith, New York, 1944

BYRD, MARTHA, *Chennault Giving Wings to the Tiger*. University of Alabama Press, 1987

CORNELIUS, WANDA, AND SHORT, THAYNE, *Ding Hao – America's Air War in China, 1937-1945*. Pelican Publishing Co, Gretna, Louisiana, 1980

DUMAS, JIM, *Longburst and the Flying Tigers*. Scrub Jay Press, Toll House, California, 2001

FRANCILLON, RENE, *Japanese Aircraft of the Pacific War*. Putnam, London, 1987

GREEN, WILLIAM, AND SWANBOROUGH, GORDON, *Japanese Army Fighters, Part Two*. Arco Publishing Co Inc, New York, 1978

HEIFERMAN, RON, *Flying Tigers – Chennault in China*. Ballantine Books Inc, New York, 1971

HILL, DAVID LEE 'TEX' WITH SCHAUPP, REAGAN, *'Tex' Hill – Flying Tiger*. The Honoribus Press, Spartanburg, South Carolina, 2003

JOHNSEN, FREDERICK A, *P-40 Warhawk*. MBI Publishing Co, Osceola, Wisconsin, 1998

KISSICK, LUTHER C, *Guerrilla One*. Sunflower University Press, Manhattan, Kansas, 1983

LITTLE, WALLACE H, *Tiger Sharks*. Castle Books, Memphis, Tennessee, 1985

LOPEZ, DONALD S, *Into the Teeth of the Tiger*. Bantam Books Inc, New York, 1986

MCCLURE, GLENN E, *Fire and Fall Back*. Barnes Press, San Antonio, Texas, 1975

MOLESWORTH, CARL, *Sharks Over China*. Brassey's, Washington, D.C., 1994

MOLESWORTH, CARL, *Osprey Aircraft of the Aces 35 – P-40 Warhawk Aces of the CBI*. Osprey Publishing, Oxford, 2000

MOLESWORTH, CARL, *Duel 8 – P-40 Warhawk vs Ki-43 'Oscar' China 1944-45*. Osprey Publishing, Oxford, 2008

MONDEY, DAVID, *Axis Aircraft of World War II*. Chancellor Press, London, 1996

OLYNYK, FRANK J, *USAAF Credits (China-Burma-India Theater) For The Destruction of Enemy Aircraft in Air-To-Air Combat World War II*. Frank J Olynyk, Aurora, Ohio, 1986

OLYNYK, FRANK J, *Stars & Bars – A Tribute to the American Fighter Ace 1920-1973*. Grub Street, London, 1995

ROSHOLT, MALCOLM, *Days of the Ching Pao*. Rosholt House, Wisconsin, 1978

ROSHOLT, MALCOLM, *Flight in the China Air Space, 1910-1950*. Rosholt House, Wisconsin, 1984

RUST, KENN C, *The Fourteenth Air Force Story*. Historical Aviation Album, Glendale, California, 1977

SAKAIDA, HENRY, *Osprey Aircraft of the Aces 13 – Japanese Army Air Force Aces 1937-45*. Osprey Publishing, Oxford, 1997

SCOTT, ROBERT L, *God Is My Co-Pilot*. Charles Scribner & Sons, New York, 1943

SHIBA, TAKEJIRO, *Japanese Monograph No 76 – Air Operations in the China Area, July 1937-August 1945*. Headquarters, USAFFE and Eighth US Army (Rear), Tokyo, 1956

SNYDER, LOUIS L, *The War – A Concise History 1939-1945*. Simon & Schuster, New York, 1960

PERIODICALS
Rabena, Oscar H, *'Japanese Air Power In The Second World War – Its Strengths and Weaknesses'*. OSS Digest, Volume 4.3, 1999

OFFICIAL UNIT HISTORIES
16th FS, 74th FS, 75th FS, 76th FS, 118th TRS, 449th FS, 23rd FG and China Air Task Force.

WEBSITES

http://www.76fsa.org

http://cbi-theater-5.home.comcast.net/roundup/roundup.html

http://cbi-theater.home.comcast.net/menu/cbi_home.html

http://www.cbi-history.com

http://www.flyingtiger.org

http://genemcguire.com

http://hawksnest.1hwy.com/In%20Service/InService.html

http://www.p40warhawk.com

http://www.sinoam.com

http://www.armyairforces.com

INDEX

References to illustrations are shown in **bold**. Colour
Plates (pl.) and Colour Section (cs.) illustrations are
shown with page and caption locators in brackets.